REFLECTIONS

&

Rhymes

REFLECTIONS

AND

RHYMES

BY

YETTA POWELL

*'If poetry comes not as naturally as the leaves to a tree
it had better not come at all°*
                                        John Keats

Published 1996 for
Reflections
London, England
Reprinted January 2000
Reprinted in January 2005
Reprinted on Amazon 2018

CONTENTS

PART THREE: LOVE

FOREWORD

As a healer and a writer of poems and short stories, I see that more and more people are becoming aware of the power of words, poetry and of thought.

Words like joy, peace and love are healing and strengthening on all levels, to the speaker, the writer, the reader and the listener.

Negative words have the opposite effect.

Those who write poetry and those who read it and/or listen to it know how therapeutic and healing it can be.

A poem, like a crystal or gem, encapsulates energy. In a few words, a mood, an emotion, a thought is created which speaks to the heart of the reader, for he himself has experienced the same feelings.

'Writing helps to connect with our inner healing self'
Gillie Bolton

'Poetry is what in a poem makes you laugh, cry, prickle, be silent, makes your toenails twinkle
Dylan Thomas

Love and joy and peace to all who read this book.
Yetta Powell

To my Teacher who inspired me.
To my husband and children and
to my adorable grandaughter Rachaet.

Rachael at 17 months

Rachael at 20 months

PART ONE

REFLECTIONS

'Life itself is our mirror'

°Man can see his reflection only when he bends down close to it; and the heart of man, too, must bear down to the heart of his fellow; then it will see itself within his heart.'

- Jewish Proverb

REFLECTIONS

Only in a mirror
Can we see our own eyes.
There's no other way.
Look deeply and see,
The true being within.
The witness, the friend, The
Lover.

Everyone we meet
Is our mirror.
In them, we see ourselves,
Our hopes, our fears,
Our worries, our faults,
And play out our dramas
On each and every one.

Life itself is our mirror.
Everything is reflected there.
Sometimes it's hard to look
And see the true reflection.
It takes honesty and courage
To keep the glass clear, And look.

TIME TO CHOOSE

It's time to choose
No compromise
No doubts
No indecision.
Time to choose,
One side or the other.
The chasm is deepening,
The divide is widening
Soon, to cross over
Will be impossible.

Which side will *you* choose?
Will you choose unconsciousness?
Half asleep, half alive,
Stumbling through life, killing time,
                                        surviving,
Uncaring, getting goods and acquisitions
Yet ever more dissatisfied.
Acting without love or moral sense
Life negating
Missing the beauty and true joy of life.

Or will you choose to live consciously,
Fulfilling your true destiny.
Learning, caring, loving
All human life and creatures on this earth.
Valuing the wonder of the gift,
Appreciating the miracle of life
Choosing what you were put on earth for
Choosing life, choosing God.

So choose now
Before it is too late
Are you to be counted
With the quick or the dead
With darkness or light?
Realise yourself, know yourself
Learn, give love, and open your heart
And give thanks to God.

RAINY DAY

'I'm saving up for a rainy day,' he said
'For when I'm old, decrepit, bent and grey,
So that I've got somewhere safe to lay my head
Food to eat, clothes, heating and a comfortable bed.

I have to work hard now, I haven't got time
To play, to look at birds and sky, trees and flowers
                                        in their prime
For the future I am working so that I will be free
One day to relax and rest and enjoy being me.'

But good, sweet man, what of the now and the life
                                        slipping past?
It won't last forever, time is going so fast.
You have to live now, to enjoy every day
To learn to just *be,* to appreciate, to play.

WHY ARE WE HERE?

We are here to love, we are here to learn, we are
                                    here to be,
And remember that our sojourn is but temporary.
Yes, there will be anguish, sorrow, but joy too,
For to experience happiness is up to you.

We look in all directions 'til we're weak and worn,
But joy's within us always from the day we're born.
The love that flows within us so abundantly free,
Just let it flow to all, whoever they may be.

Give love to friends and strangers, everyone you meet,
The small child crying, feeble lady in the street.
Your wife, your husband, children, family,
Just everyone needs love so desperately.

Give love to animals who give us so much,
Give love with words, a smile, a look, a touch.
Give love with hugs and kisses, laughter too,
And please remember to give love to *you*

Love must be sincere and true and given free,
It will return a thousand fold as you will see.

GO FOR JOY

Go for joy! that's what it's all about.
Just laugh and sing and smile and dance and shout.
 Let's see each day as a big celebration
Just look and marvel at the whole creation.

Let's listen to the blackbird's thrilling song.
He sings his praises to God all day long.
Just see those roses bursting into flower.
They gladly give their perfume hour by hour.

And look at babies and their eyes so bright
So full of love and joy and life and light.
And children playing, limbs so free and lithe.
So full of joy, and happy just to be alive.

Then what of grief and suffering, pain and sighs?
But joy is there always; open up your eyes!
The way people do not see is just incredible
That each of us is such a miracle.

Instead of grumbling, try appreciation
Open up your heart to exaltation.
Let love and beauty be your inspiration
And joy flow through you with exhilaration.

A SHINING JEWEL AWAITS

In this crazy jungle
That we all create,
Within - a shining jewel
For us to find - awaits.

Its name is truth!
Its glory ever burning.
When we look for happiness,
It is for truth we're yearning.

Some call it Love or Peace or God,
Or Infinite Energy.
We look for it in every place,
Except where it may be.

But when were tired of searching
In every place on Earth,
We're shown that precious diamond
That's been with us from birth.

WHY DON'T WE CARE ANYMORE?

Why don't we care anymore?
Why don't we care anymore?
When an old man is mugged and cries 'Help me!'
We're all as busy as can be
When some poor soul falls to the ground,
We avert our eyes and walk around.
Yes, we close our eyes to another's need.
The focus today is on wants and on greed.

Why don't we care anymore?
Why don't we care anymore?
For the suffering of animals who should live free,
Defenceless, depending on you and on me.
For Third World children starving to death,
For the aborted unborn not allowed to take breath.
Disease and famine, murderous rage.
Does it not merit more than a newspaper page?

Why don't we care anymore?
Why don't we care anymore?
Are we so hardened to blood, violence and war,
That we just don't notice it any more?
We turn off that channel on TV.
And make another cup of tea.
We could care much more for the sick, lonely and lame
One day, who knows, we could be the same.

So Why don't we care anymore?
Why don't we care anymore?

A TINY PLANET

We live on a tiny planet
Spinning in space
In a vast Universe
Of countless, infinite Universes
And numberless planets and
stars.
We are tiny and fragile,
And infinitely finite.

Yet we humans
Segregate ourselves
Into groups, into religions,
Each one feeling
Theirs is the right one, the only one,
That they will be saved
And all the others condemned to *Hell*.

How arrogant we are.
As Jews, as Christians,
Moslems, Buddhists and all the others
Too many to count.
Can't we see how the differences
Divide us from each other
Creating discord, hate and war?

We are all human beings
Living from breath to breath
With the same needs and desires,
Experiencing the same birth and death.
We have to learn to live together
In harmony and love
On this tiny beautiful planet spinning in the
vastness of space.

HUMAN BEINGS

Shabby poor old man
Shuffling down the street,
Pushing a rusting cart,
Battered slippers on feet.

Grizzled, tired face,
Hands so gnarled and worn,
Grubby old cap on head,
Shapeless coat all torn.

What does he think
As he slowly wends his way,
Will he get some food
And perhaps a drink today?

Ragged poor old man
Existing on this Earth
Once too, he was a baby
Some woman gave him birth.

Did his mother hold him?
Was he her love and joy?
Was his father full of pride
For his son, his boy?

Did he grow to childhood,
Happy and free from care,
Joyful to wake up each day.
What has brought him here?

Spruce, smart business man
Striding down the street.
Pin stripes and umbrella
Well shined shoes on feet.

On his way to daily work
To the great *rat race*
With warm fat stomach replete
And bland, unsmiling face.

Passing by the old man
Without a second glance
Does he reflect for a second
That it could be himself by chance?

Passing by each other
They live in world's apart.
Yet each is a breathing being,
With life and a human heart.

All share the same life on this Earth,
Whether we're rich or poor.
All share the same way of birth,
And leave at the same door.

MIND AND HEART

My mind said 'No!'

My heart said 'Go!'

My mind said 'Let's see'

My heart said 'I need to be free'

My mind said 'It's a ploy°'

My hearts said 'Just enjoy'

My mind said 'Are you sure?'

My heart said 'It will endure'

My mind said 'Yes - but - '

My heart said 'I'll not stay in that rut°'

My mind said 'My problems bring me low'

My heart said 'They will always come and go°'

My mind said 'I have other things to do°'

My heart said 'I only want what's true°'

My mind said 'It's unreal'

My heart said 'Reality is what you feel'

My mind said 'I just don't understand'

My heart said 'You never will, it's a wonderland.'

MY TEMPLE

My Temple is not made of gold
Of granite, wood or stone,
To its peace, alone,
I enter But never am I alone.

My Temple is not far away,
I do not travel there to be.
I can go within at any time
It's closer than my breath to me.

My Temple is more precious,
Than diamonds, pearls or gold,
It is as new as each bright dawn,
And countless ages old.

SO GOOD

The wind was fierce

I was cold and wet

The skies were sad and grey - and yet -

Within my heart I felt *so good*

So safe and warm as I know I should.

SAFE HARBOUR

My boat has found its harbour,
I no longer need to roam,
My anchor is strong and sure and firm,
And I am safely home.

For years my boat had drifted,
In perilous seas forlorn.
I was lost and without direction,
And felt so much alone.

I searched the seas to find a place,
Where my journey at last could end,
I cried for help and looked in vain,
For the appearance of a friend.

I could have been smashed on the rocks,
Or washed far out to sea,
And never know why I was here,
Or how wonderful life can be.

But now the harbour master,
Has come to rescue me,
And shown me a sea of peace and calm,
As my journey is meant to be.

WAKE UP!

Are you still asleep
When so much magic is around?
Are your open eyes really closed
Are you deaf to every sound?

Wake up! wake up! and listen!
While you are still on this
Earth It is no accident,
That you were given birth.

There is an inner truth
That you were meant to find,
A pure beauty and love within.
But so many to it are blind.

ANGEL

Did I dream or imagine
A gentle presence
The whisper of a whisper
The brush of a wing
A heavenly fragrance
A comforting, a love
An enfolding
Was it a dream?

Oh how I wish I could see you!

LISTENING TO MY HEART

I cannot follow blindly
As others seem to do
But only listen to my heart
And do what it tells me to.

Let's strip away the layers
The fantasy, hype and pride
And try to be always true to ourselves
Let our own hearts be our guide.

WE ARE ALL HEALERS

We are all healers, each in our own way,
Whatever it is that we do every day
The compassion of a mother for the child she loves so much
Her soft voice, her selfless love, and her gentle touch.

The nurse is a healer and plays her part,
With constant attention and caring heart.
The lover heals with his caress,
With his soft words and tenderness.

A true friend will heal with words so kind,
To help to ease a troubled mind.
We don't have to lay on hands to heal our fellow man
We just have to do our work the best that we can.

LONELINESS

We pass each other in the street,
But, never a glance, a smile, a response.
Some young, some old, some middle aged,
All carrying baskets, bags or holdalls
On their way to the shops
Or on their way back.
We're all like little islands,
Wrapped up in ourselves,
Like our groceries
Closed up on ourselves
Like the front doors we shut on our return.

RIPPLES

Like a pebble
Dropped in a lake,
If I send out a little love
A little healing,
The ripples will expand
And take it further and further,
I know not where,
And I do not need to know.

MEDITATION

When you feel
Depressed and lonely,
And really you just want
To hide,
If you can try
Some meditation,
God will smile at you inside.

Your body may not be so perfect, And your mind full
of anxiety, But if you go within yourself, You will feel
peace, you will be free!

YOUR HEART SPOKE TO MY HEART

It doesn't matter
What you said,
For your heart spoke
To my heart.

It doesn't matter
What was left unsaid,
For your heart spoke
To my heart.

INSTRUMENTS

We all think we are the conductors,
The conductors of the orchestra,
But that we are not.
We're not even the conductor of our own little
                                              instruments,
Be it sweet flute, deep bassoon or mellow cello.
We wave our baton, our feeble arms,
And think we can control the whole world,
And bring in each instrument as we will,
At our speed, at our pitch,
And blend them, mix them as we wish,
To make one glorious, successful orchestration.
But it doesn't work that way,
Although maybe it seems that way for some.
It may work out the way they want *now,*
But I see it isn't up to us,
We didn't write the music or the score,
And we didn't make the instruments,
We *are* the instruments.

BOATS

Our little boats sail on the sea of life,
The way ends and begins at the same source.
And travelling, they meet fair winds and foul,
Sweet gentle breezes and great hurricanes of force.

Sometimes they gently rock upon the waves,
And drink the sweetly nectar scented air
But often they are torn and tossed about
Until the sails are ripped and keel laid bare.

Upon the ocean, they meet other craft,
Some big, some small, all on the journey bent,
And some are modest with a tiny sail.,
And others gaudy and extravagant.

We pass each other on the way,
And some perhaps we'll never see again.
And others sail quite near for many a mile,
And some we try to keep with might and main.

But have no fear about the other craft,
Even though each one alone to make the journey must.
For every boat has love and shelter all the way,
So traveller, sail the sea of life with courage, hope and
                                                    trust.

PEACE

I see peace in the tiny baby fast asleep.

Peace in the sheep grazing quietly on the hill.

Peace in the silvery moonlight softly shining down,

As by the weeping willow I stand still.

Peace in the murmuring stream flowing thru' the fields.

Peace in the sweet, fresh, fragrant early morn.

Peace in the diamond dew that sparkles on the grass.

Peace in each pure creature newly born.

Peace in the gentle doves cooing overhead.

Peace in the bright eyed blackbird singing in the tree.

The peace we experience in this world

Reflects the true peace within you, within me.

GET ON WITH IT!

If there's something
You want to do
Get on with it!
Don't say you
Haven't got the time
This is all the time
You've got
Don't blame others
For stopping you
Only you
Can stop you
You can do anything
You want
If you really want
To do it
So get on with it!

WHY?

How cruel to see that once strong body, now so frail,
Those hands, once firm, now weak,
Those eyes, once bright and confident,
Lips that can barely speak.

Long, long ago, he was a happy child,
He ran and laughed, the young blood rushing free.
The years of work and worry take their toll.
Why does this have to be?'

Why can't we be born old, and then die young?
Why can't we laugh at death, as at birth we cry?
Only God Himself knows the mystery
Of why we live and die.

FRIENDSHIP

How many friends
Do we have in our time?
We think we have dozens
When we're in our prime.

Friends made while at school,
At our work, at our play,
But how many of these
Do we still have today?

Everything changes,
And people do too
One day they are friendly,
And the next ignore you.

Like ships on the ocean,
They come and they go,
That's what happens in life
So no need to feel low.

A few friends will stick
Through thick and through thin,
But the truest friend of all
Is the one that's within.

SUCCESS

Where the world's concerned, my life is quite a mess
In no way, can you call me a success.
No fame or fortune whatever can I leave.
No book has my name printed on its sleeve.
No plane, no boat, no villa in the south,
No operatic aria ever filled my mouth.
I never had Elizabeth Taylor's looks,
And you'll not find me in the History books.

But I've seen glorious sunsets.
I've heard the blackbird sing.
I've held three babies in my arms,
Breathed the fragrance of each spring.
I've seen mountains, rivers, lakes so blue,
Felt the power of the sea,
Exchanged love and kisses, tears and smiles,
Seen the seasons change a tree.
I've tasted sweet fruits of all kinds,
Felt the sun, the wind, the rain.
I've walked and danced and laughed and sung,
I have not lived in vain.

And I have breathed that radiance,
Touched those feet,
And seen that loving smile
Incredibly sweet.
No matter if not rich or famous or a star, God
truly loves us as we really are.

ONIONS

We are all like onions,
With layers and layers and layers and layers,
Some onions are bigger,
And some layers are tougher,
But they all have to be peeled away
Until nothing is left but the essence.
It's a bit painful when layers are stripped away
But it has to be.

A baby is like a little spring onion,
No layers, just sweetness and tenderness.
Then, the layers start to grow.
We have to protect ourselves,
Make our defences against the world,
Parents, teachers, happenings, plaster layers on us,
Until as time goes by -
We become tough old onions,
With lots of layets,
And papery brown skins.

When I peel an onion it makes me cry,
And when I get peeled, I feel like crying too But
it's not all painful,
Because under all the layers,
And layers and layers and layers and layers, Is the
real true me, the real sweet you.

I'LL NOT DWELL

I'll not dwell futilely
On the past
And what might
Have been,
For doubt and remorse
And regret,
Can no longer be my scene.

Neither do I wish
To speculate,
On what the future
Will bring,
But live each day
Fully and with
Consciousness,
And allow my heart to sing.

ONE DAY

One day the sun will rise
But not for me.
One day the moon will shine
But not for me.

One day the rain will fall
And I'll not feel it.
One day the birds will sing
And I'll not hear it.

But *now* the sky and sea exist for me,
The birds sing, the sun shines just for me.
The flowers bloom, the cherry trees blossom just for me.
All the treasures of the world are there for me.

And now I can enjoy and taste and hear and see
And feel the joy and wonder of this space andtime.
Each breath reminds me that I am here now,
Each day a new beginning, a new life.

SOMETIMES

Sometimes, I wish I was a tree,
So strong, so true, so full of grace,
Lifting its arms towards the sky
In a glorious, leafy, green embrace.

Sometimes, I wish I was a bird
With feathery wings soaring in the sky,
Filling the earth with sweet harmonies.
It must feel wonderful to fly.

Sometimes, I wish I was a rose
The symbol of a loving heart,
With wondrous fragrance, colour, beauty,
The Creator's gift of divine art.

Sometimes, I wish I was the sea
That ebbs and flows so constantly.
Strange creatures dwell within its depths
An awe inspiring mystery.

But I'm glad, I'm glad that I am me,
Appreciating the gifts in the world so side,
With the life and consciousness given me,
Feeling the true beauty that dwells inside.

The tree, the bird, the rose, the sea,
All have the same life energy.
Different we seem, but we are one,
For from the same Source we have come.

OUR WORLD

This is the world God has made.
This is the world God has made.
Pure clear water in full measure,
Fresh fragrant air, the greatest treasure.
To warm and refresh us, sun, wind and rain.
Herbs of all kinds to ease our pain.
Fruits, so delicious for all to share.
Other human beings for whom to care.
Animals to comfort us and help our work hours.
Beautiful scents and hues of so many flowers.
Birds singing sweetly from dawn 'til night
The gifts of body and brain, hearing and sight.

This is the world man has made.
This is the world man has made.
Polluted air not fit to breathe.
Water so poisoned, it begins to seethe.
Sun hidden by smoke and acid rain.
Earth become desert never to grow again.
Medicines to cure that are in vain.
Man killing man - the curse of Cain.
Children starving while food's thrown away.
People in fear of destruction every day.
Animals in cages living only to die,
Fruits sprayed with chemicals by planes in the sky
Greed and power and lust and hate.
We must learn to care, before it's too late.

ST ALBAN ABBEY

A golden edifice of stone
Rising with sublime grace to the sky.
Myriads of feet have trodden here.
You have seen multitudes live and die.

Thick with old world History,
The air is still and grave.
Through the glory of stained glass, sunlight glows
And shines down on the nave.

The choirboys in their long, red gowns
Lift voices pure and sweet.
A place of quiet to meditate
A peacefulness complete.

CAN'T YOU SEE?

Can't you see
How wonderful you are?

Can't you feel
The miracle of being alive?

Can't you see True
reality?

Listen to me!
The world is beautiful
But only if you first find
The beauty within yourself.

HUMAN BEINGS 2

We are human beings
We are human
We are human beings
But are we really?
We are always doing, doing, doing, doing
And hardly ever just being, being, being

Rushing here and there
Filling every moment
Feeling guilt by not being busy, busy, busy
Going here and there, doing this and that
Feeling false pride and ego at all the things
We can do at the same time

Animals are beautiful beings
They just are, just themselves
If not doing anything
They sleep and play and eat
And sometimes do nothing at all

Babies and children are true beings
Always in the moment
Focusing on one thing at a time
All is wonder, all is joy
And people become more being
As they get older.

PAST HISTORY

The tears unshed
The words unsaid
The love denied
The high held pride
The hopes, the fears
Through the long years
So let it be
Past history.

UNIQUE PERFORMANCE

So here we are!
This is the stage
The actors are you and I
Living, breathing, sentient beings.
The time is now;
No rehearsals,
No encores,
So enjoy the play,
This - is - *it!*

So enjoy the play,
Play the music,
Dance to the rhythm,
Sing the praises,
The glory, the majesty,
Of the producer
The director, the puppeteer.
Live it, love it
Learn it, enjoy it!

It's just a short play,
For there are infinite others to be performed,
Many actors, many roles
To come and go.
So enjoy *your* play
You may laugh, you may cry
But feel it, experience it
It will never be performed again
One unique, solo performance.

THE CREATOR CREATES

The Creator creates,
The believer believes,
Peace is the want of all men,
But only those who believe that this realisation
                                        is the ultimate
Will find this wanted *Peace*.

Trust Him, for He will show you,
All other things are immaterial,
They never last,
But, this will last forever.

Your body is but a shell,
But, this shell must be kept from harm,
For inside this shell there is something that
must be loved,
From this love, comes love for others,
This love is life, happiness and *Peace*.

(Written by Sharon Powell at age 15)

L'CHAIM - TO LIFE

Well my dear child
How did you find your time on Earth?
And what did you experience from your birth?
Did you feel love, did you feel joy?
Did you understand you were there to learn and enjoy?

Well dear Father
I learned a great deal, often through pain
And tried not to repeat my mistakes again
I learned when I gave love, it came back to me
I learned to express my given creativity

There were so many things for me to explore
And so much to feel, hear, see and adore
I learned to be in touch with You within me
And found there peace, joy and true reality

Yes it was an adventure, a wonderful show
So thank you, it was glorious as I'm sure you will know.

CLASSROOM

The faces look up
In trust and expectancy,
Eagerness and friendship
In the eyes.
Eyes bright
With life and hope,
The faces look up
Each one unique,
Colours, shapes,
Movement and expression
Merge,
Then reappear as individuals.
Character and personality forming
Here is the embryo.
Living material,
To be made or marred.

YOU HAVE ALL THE ANSWERS!

We spend so much time
Asking this one and that one,
Why? How? And what should I do?
But all the wisdom and answers you need,
Are there, yes, right within you.

SOME PEOPLE

Some people get old as they get older,
But you get younger.
Some people get worse as they get older,
But you get better.
Some people get cross and sour,
But you get kinder and sweeter.
Some people's hearts close up like clams,
But yours is more open with love.
Some people grow rigid with their concepts,
But you are more clear and aware.
Some people get selfish and self centred,
But you get more caring.
My love
I think you're wonderful!

SOCIAL RESPECTABILITY

Social Respectability
Doesn't have to be,
But prepare to face ridicule,
If you want to bend the rules,
For you can't expect to grow
If you never can say 'No.'

TIME -1

Time is very patient
He does not grasp.
He knows that all will come to him at last.

Time is always there
And he can wait.
He knows that all will pass, it is our fate.

The massive skyscrapers' steel
Will eventually rust
And the great pyramids of Egypt
Will turn to dust

TIME - 2

In time, Time will claim all, He has us all from our
birth Back to the elements everything will go
Fire, water, air and earth.

FREE WILL

We point the finger
And cry
How could they do that?
I couldn't do that!

Are you sure?
Within us lives God,
And demons also,
If we allow.

A little higher than the animals,
A little lower than the angels,
And free will.
We can choose.

We are all responsible,
We cannot judge,
We are the victims,
And also the perpetrators

We are all one.

A GENTLE REMINDER

As healers, ever grateful
We really need to be,
For we are living channels
And need humility.

Graced to be healers,
Let's do the best we can,
Be conscious of what we say and do, To
help our fellow man.

Let's remember just why we are here,
With love and integrity,
Not criticise or focus,
On triviality.

We cannot look at others,
And judge the work they do,
Only God knows everyone's true worth,
Its not up to me or you.

LITTLE CHILD

Little child, little one,
Smiling up at me,
With such a sweetness.
Discovering your fingers
With wonder,
Sucking your toes,
Kicking and gurgling,
Completely at home.
Completely happy.
Filling me with love,
As if you were mine.

Little miracle.
You show me,
That life is our friend.
Benevolent, smiling, welcoming.
That we are here to enjoy,
And feel the joy within us.
That we can feel safe,
And never be afraid,
For life loves us,
And give us all we need,
Freely, magnificently, magically.

BRIGHT FEATHERS

With bright feathers I fly
To the sun, to the sky
Gleaming, incandescent, exultantly,
Freely I fly, wings outstretched in joy.

I sing from my heart,
Throat throbbing, gratefully, a glorious song
Of exhilaration, of the air,
Rising swiftly past my wings.

With other birds, I fly,
Singing of life, of wonder,
Of bliss and freedom,
Air, wind and breath.

I did not know one day,
A hunter would find and capture me,
To keep my beauty for his own,
And hold me pinioned to his breast.

Trembling, fearful, struggling in vain,
I lost consciousness,
And when life returned
Found myself in a cage of gold.

A tiny space, bars surrounding me,
In terror, I beat my wings and body
Against the cold bright metal,
Vainly to reach the sky again.

In vain I beat and cried
'Til my body bruised and bleeding,
Exhausted I lay on the floor,
Resigned piteously to my fate.

I have food, I have water,
I have warmth, I am safe.
Humans come, to admire me
'How beautiful,' they say in wonder.

But still within, I see the sky,
Hear the wild birds singing,
As they fly to the stars.
How happy they are.

One day my bird within
Will fly away,
Will soar to the skies
And again I will be free.

WHY WAS I BORN?

Why was I born?
Why am I here?
What must I do?
What is my destiny?

The face looks up
Wide eyes questioningly with trust.
So many questions,
So many choices,
So many roads.
So many *should's* or *must.*

Little one - it's so simple,
The answers are within you,
You were born to love,
To learn, to help, to know,
To grow, to be and to enjoy,
Love is your destiny.

THIS HOUSE

This house
Once filled with noise
And children and laughter
Reawakens to you ---
Rachael
With your joy and your smile
Your sense of fun
Your constant activity
And your first words and sounds

YET STILL

The storm rages,
The wind blows fiercely,
The thunder crashes,
Yet still the sun shines through.

The angry words,
The fear, mistrust,
The doubts, the guilt,
Yet still the good shines through.

The greed, the violence,
The war, the pestilence,
The misery, the poverty,
Yet still the love shines through.

PRAYER AFTER MEDITATION

Lord -

May I remember you with every breath,

May I see you in everyone and everything,

And feel you always in my heart.

SOCIALLY CORRECT

Whatsoever troubles
You are going through,
You may feel sad,
You may feel blue.
But no matter how much you may object,
You must be socially correct.

You smile,
Though you feel sad inside.
Pull down the blinds on your face,
And hide inside.
Pretend to be OK to keep the world's respect,
For you really must be socially correct.

HEALING

I feel gratitude and awe.
That I am trusted to heal,
And to listen to others,
And hear how they feel.

Inside each is a little child,
A vulnerable being,
When the healing channels through me,
Their true nature I'm seeing.

I see that everyone is filled with love,
Though perhaps they don't yet know,
Until they experience through healing
That this really is so.

MOTHER'S DAY

I look at them
Sitting round the table,
Tall and big and handsome.
Discussing shares,
And computers,
And work,
And the Internet.
It's a foreign language to me.

I look at them,
And remember the babies, I
carried and changed and fed.
The toddlers I kept amused,
The children I took to school.
The Brownies, the Cubs, The
birthday teas.
The school friends.

I vaguely remember
The rebellions,
The hair, the loud music.
House full of young people,
Trying this thing and that.
The joys and the tears,
The relationships that didn't work
And those that did.

And this is Mother's Day.
They have come bearing flowers and cards,
And I am filled with pride and joy,
As I look at my three children,
Grown from babies to adults,
Creative and caring, intelligent and
enterprising,
Loving and independent
And I am grateful.

TO RACHAEL (AT 5 MONTHS)

Little baby
Little girl
How beautiful you are
Your lovely smile
Lights up my heart
Your eyes are like the stars

You show me
What life really means In
your simplicity Your delight
and wonder At everything
Are such a joy to me.

Everything you see and hear
Is a delight
To you
A tree, a flower,
A bird, the sky
You see with eyes so new.

I hope
You'll always keep this joy
And wonder you have each day
And appreciate the lovely gifts you have
And enjoy your life always.

DO YOU REALISE

Do you realise
That we live
From breath to breath?
That within each
And every breath
We experience
Both life and death?

We take each breath
For granted
As we naturally inhale
But we are very temporary
And we are very frail

Every breath
Is given
To each one of us
Throughout our lives
Lets be grateful
And appreciate
The one who lets us thrive.

SOMETIMES

Sometimes I feel your presence,
And sometimes I don't.
Sometimes I feel your love,
And sometimes not.
But, - like the clouds
That cover the sun,
Which is always shining anyway,
I guess its the clouds of my mind,
                    That hide you from me.

BELIEF

You may not believe in God,
But God believes in you,
And will hold you in his arms,
Lovingly, your whole life through.

He was there at the beginning,
And will be there at the end,
He lives always in your heart,
And is your dearest, truest friend.

He will never leave you,
Alone you are - never!
And despite your disbelief
(Dear brother). He will be there forever!

REBIRTH

A new beginning
All fears, resentments
Cut away
All guilt, negativity
Have gone today

A new chance to live
And to enjoy
Each breath, each day
With love and joy.

THESE THINGS ARE FREE

These things are free -
The sparkling stars,
The sky above,
The dewy grass,
Friendship and love.
Mountains, lakes, rivers,
Sunsets, moonshine,
The dawn, the morning air
Sweeter than wine.
The air, the water,
Autumnal trees,
Sweet smelling roses
Butterflies, honey bees.
The storm, the rainbow,
Refreshing sleep,
The song 'of birds,
A memory to keep.
The hoot of owls,
The dove's sweet coo,
Incredible free gifts from God,
For me and for you.
The smiles, the laughter,
The tears that sometimes flow.
The voice within that whispers,
'My child, I know, I know.'

IF THE WORLD WERE TO END

If the world were to end
Tomorrow
Just how would you spend
Your last day
Would you view it as just a normal day
Would you spend it at work or at play?

Would you spend it in meditation and prayer
Be with crowds or in solitude
Or eat your fill of every food
And get as drunk as you possibly could

Would you tell your family that you dearly love them
And say good-bye to your friends
Would you tear up your will and shred all your bills
Forgive all, and make your amends

The end of the world is not imminent
Despite what Nostradamus said in his day
But the end of our World will come of course
For one day we must leave any way.

HEAVEN

If you're good
You'll go to Heaven,
But - if you're bad
You'll go to Hell!
Every Sunday on TV.
They thunder and hammer it in so well.

They base their faith,
On fear and guilt,
And pour
Their message in.
That God is revengeful and will punish,
And is recording every sin.

But you just watch
A baby,
Or a little child's
Shining eyes,
To know that Heaven is within,
And not up there in the skies.

SLOW DOWN

Slow down!
No need to rush
Unless you want to get caught
In the crush

Take your time
Relax and rest
Your body will be grateful
And your mind be at its best

Enjoy and smell the flowers
As you go
Don't miss out on all the wonders
For you to know

If you try to do too much
Each day and every day
You will really meet yourself
Coming back the other way!

So savour each sweet moment
Instead of doing, doing, you just be
All will get done in time
Slow down and you will see.

PART TWO

RHYMES

'Let the sense and rhyme always agree'

Nicholas Brileau

CHICKEN SOUP

Childhood memories remain, wheresoever I rove,
Of the chicken soup simmering on the stove.
Oh the wafting of that fragrant smell!
The delicious taste - I remember it well.
Through births, barmitzvahs, weddings too,
And all the traumas we went through,
The chicken soup was there for all,
The old, the babies, the big the small.
A bereavement, a fever, a headache, the croup,
The cure for them all was my Mum's chicken soup.
On Friday night we were more than willing,
To enjoy a full plate of Jewish penicillin.

ALTERNATIVE HYPOCHONDRIA

I woke up this morning feeling tense and depressed
Wondering what I could do, 'twas too soon to get dressed.
So, I tried Dr Bach, Kali Phos, Herbal Kalms,
Gave my feet Reflexology and recited some Psalms
Visualised myself as peaceful, did some strong Affirmations,
Tried Self-Hypnosis and Yoga and practiced Meditation.
Also Acupressure, Touch for Health, and Aromatherapy,
Tried Alexander Method
And drank some Rooibosch Tea.

WISHES

I'd love to see a kingfisher diving to catch fish.
To see some funny puffins, is another wish.
To see elephants roaming wild would be a great delight,
And humming birds and lions and tigers burning bright.
I'd like to see that Haley's Comet shoot across the sky.
I'd love to hold my grandchild and watch him smile and cry
I want to visit India and view the Taj Mahal,
And then to tour round China and see the old Great Wall.
I wish I could write incredible books.
I wish I'd been born with stunning looks.
I wish I could create a work of art.
I wish I could express the love in my heart.
I wish I had lots of money so I could give some away
And then go to Harrods and have a real field day.
I wish all the world's children could always happy be
Feel safe and loved, well fed and clothed
Within a family
I really wish all people could learn to live together
In peace and love and harmony, for ever and forever.

FOOD FOR THOUGHT

If I don't control my mind,
My mind controls me,
And will fill me full
Of negativity.

After all, who wants to feel
Depressed, sad and awful,
When you can choose to be,
Happy, glad and cheerful.

In France, in the 17th century lived
A philosopher, a very wise man,
Called Rene Descartes, who said we're told
'I think, therefore I am!'

The answer to his existence,
Is what it seems he sought,
But the truth is that what we are right now Is
what we have ever thought.

DON'T LOOK BACK

Don't look back
Along the track
That you trod
So long ago
For you can't change it
Or exchange it
It's a no - no
So let it go.

WE ARE FORTUNATE

It seems quite cool
That if a wasp
Is buzzing in our room

We'll swat it hard
Without a qualm
And send it to its doom.
And yet *we* are so fortunate
With the mess we've made all round
That a gigantic foot doesn't just come down
And squash *us* to the ground.

HOLISTIC THERAPY

Here comes the age of holistic therapy
When for ourselves we take full responsibility,
When a person is seen as body, mind and soul,
And not treated in bits, but as a complete whole.

Acupuncture, Alexander, Radionics, Healing,
Reflexology and Aromatherapy can give you a
good feeling
Homeopathy, Osteopathy, one will fit you like
a glove
The names may be different, but they all work
with love.

I'D LIKE

I'd like to be a puppy
Nestling in your arms,
Though tiny, weak and helpless
I'd feel so safe from harm.

I'd like to be a little bird,
I'd fly to you with speed,
And tell you that I love you,
For you've given me all I need.

I'd like to be an angel,
And sing your praises all day long,
With lutes and flutes and harps and bells,
To accompany my song.

I'd like to always feel the love,
You have for me always,
To warm me every second,
Of all my nights and days.

MACROBIOTICS

You may think it's idiotic
To eat macrobiotic
But after a while
It becomes quite hypnotic.

The Japanese names
Make it sound so exotic,
It's interesting food
But no way it's erotic.

I must keep it simple
Or I could get neurotic
Or Heaven forbid
Become quite psychotic!
Help!

SKIN DEEP

Revlon and Rubenstein
Max Factor and Rimmel,
I've used them all in my time
And yes, I know them well!

Estee Lauder and Yardley Coty,
 Ponds and Roc
Your tantalising packaging
Makes me run amok.

Lotions and potions
Powders, blushers too
Inky black mascara
Eye shadows, green and blue.

They're smashing
You feel dashing
But beneath,
You're the same old you!

Lipsticks in coral
Lipsticks in brown
There's red ones and pink ones
And shiny ones for town.

Pearly nail varnish
And perfume so balmy
And eye liner to make you
Look like Mata Hari!

GOING ON HOLIDAY

Going on holiday is such a hassle
Wouldn't it be better to stay at home?
No hectic packing, shopping or queuing,
At airports or customs.
Why does one roam?

Well - to see other views, people and places,
To experience the unusual,
Is the reason I guess.
And is it exciting?
And is it interesting?
And is it worthwhile?
Well the answer is - Yes!
And yet.. .

To sit in the garden
And drink home brewed tea,
In the shade of the Willow
With the cat on my knee.
To watch the flowers blossom,
And the leaves on the tree,
And listen to the blackbird's song,
Is pure Heaven to me!

ENGLISH WEATHER

In Miami, it gets too hot,
In England, often hot it's not.

In the UK, there's rain galore,
In Africa, they would like much more.

In most places, there are two seasons,
In England, there are many reasons,

To talk of the weather every day,
For it changes hourly, and the sun doesn't stay.

Rain, sun, thunder, snow, in twenty four hours -
It confuses the birds and the bees, and the flowers.

So since we can survive the weather here,
I guess we are tough, and could live anywhere.

FIRST KISS

We think you're very clever
A bright little miss
For you gave grandpa and grandma
A lovely sloppy kiss (your first ones ever).

DON'T JUDGE A BOOK BY ITS COVER

The eyes may wear thick black eye liner,
And masses of shadow above,
But from out of them if you look clearly,
Shines a soul that is desperate for love.

If you only just glance at a face,
And judge the hair and the clothes that are worn,
You never will see the real person inside,
Who may be with anguish torn.

We judge everyone that we meet
By the face that they choose to show,
But within is a vulnerable being
Who needs love much more than we know.

ENCHANTING

Enchanting, lovely little girl
With big brown eyes and hair that curls
You are full of love and fun
And bring joy to everyone.

IF

If there is only one life
Tell me then how it can be
That some are rich as Croesus
And others live in poverty?
That some can live for a hundred years
While others die at birth
Some live a happy, healthy life
Others in dire misery on this Earth?

WHEN I HELP OTHERS

When I help others
I really help myself
When I make you feel good
I feel good myself

When I give healing
I heal myself
When I smile at others
I receive many smiles

And when I give love
Love returns to me
And flows through me
Like an endless river.

CARS

It all began
A few months back
The Red Volvo's clapped out
(He said) Alas and Alack!

(I said) What sort of car do you fancy?
He answered with a smile
Well one that doesn't cost too
much
And hasn't done many miles.

A Rolls Royce really would be nice
A Mercedes? really?
Well! A Saab or a BMW
Or an Audi would be swell.

Now what can we get
To replace our red friend
There's cars everywhere
And makes without end.

(He said) I've been to the dealers
And scoured the newspapers
through
But I still haven't found
A car that will do.

(I said) Well I hope you will
finally
Make up your mind
And I do hope it will be soon
Before the car becomes obsolete
And we're flying off to the moon.

GAMES

Well folks, I guess the game's played out,
No longer it's a winner
For him to bring the money home
And for her to make the dinner.

ANGELS

Angels come in many forms,
And always in disguise,
You may surely recognise one,
If you open up your eyes.

The stray cat looking for a home,
The beggar in the street,
Perhaps your next door neighbour,
Indeed anyone you meet.

The cheery milkman with your milk,
The treasure who cleans your floor,
That may be a real life angel
Who is knocking at your door.

They may not have a halo,
Or wear gold shining wings,
But they could well be angels,
If they make your heart dance and sing.

So if we could only treat everyone we meet As
an angel potentially,
Instead of with suspicion,
How much happier we all could be.

TO VIVIEN AND MARTIN

I sat in your beautiful garden
Absorbing the peace and the quiet,
Enjoying the shrubs and the trees and the flowers
Red, pink, blue, yellow and white.

The branches were swaying so gently
In a soft and mild warm breeze,
The air seemed perfumed and fragrant,
By the grass and the flowers and trees.

The sky was so clear and an azure blue
Not a single white cloud to be found.
It was silent and tranquil and peaceful,
Just Birdsong and no other sound.

I watered your beautiful garden
So it happily could survive,
All the plants drank and seemed so grateful
And have continued to grow and to thrive.

In the trees, a blackbird sang sweetly
And a cheeky robin redbreast hopped near.
I heard the sound of the woodpecker
But I just didn't see any deer!

HAVE I GOT PROBLEMS

I've got problems, problems
Problems on every hand.
Problems, problems, problems, problems
Problems that I can't stand.

I've got social problems, financial problems
Problems that won't go away,
Problems, problems, problems, problems
Problems that turn your hair grey.

I've got physical problems, metaphysical problems,
Problems with my mind.
Economic problems, supersonic problems
Problems with things I can't find.

I've got problems with my body,
Aches and pains.
Arthritis, cystitis
Varicose veins.

Mental problems
Claustrophobia.
Confusion, delusions
Agoraphobia.

Problems, problems -
My problem is that
I've got problems.

DRESS SHOP

'Oh Madam you look lovely!'
When you know you look a mess
What purgatory we go through,
When we decide to buy a dress.

I just want something simple,
A lovely colour too
Please don't show me puce or purple,
Beads or bangles or frou frou.

You look at your reflection
With a shudder and some sighs,
Those scraggy, scrawny shoulders
Those bulging hips and thighs!

Then mesmerised by flattery
You settle for the red.
Then you shut it in the wardrobe,
And fall exhausted into bed!

THE HAPPY GAS

I dreamt that bombs were falling all around,
Exploding in the air and on the ground,
But nobody got hurt or blown in half,
To my surprise, no cries, no, only laughs.
For, in every bomb, no danger was inside,
But filled instead with heavy nitrous oxide,
Not hydrogen or atomic, but laughing gas -
As people streamed into the streets en masse,
And as the substance hit the ground and dust,
Just everyone started laughing fit to bust.
They laughed and laughed, 'til it became a roar
And all felt happier than they ever did before.

The laughter grew and grew, 'twas Heaven sent,
'Til it even reached the home of Parliament.
The ministers were talking in despair
Of war, and threats, and violence everywhere,
When the gas penetrated even this solemn hall
And MPs started on the floor to fall,
And roll about and clutch their sides with mirth,
And gasp 'Oh what a funny, lovely Earth -
Who wants to talk such nonsense?
Let's be merry,
Let's dance and laugh and sing, be happy - very!'
And even in the Lords, those persons proud,
Just lost their dignity and laughed so loud.

In all the prisons, doors were opened wide,
Convicts and warders, dancing jigs, could be espied.
And in the hospitals, as the gas reached the nostrils,
Doctors and patients threw away their pills.
Smiling specialists did cartwheels round the beds,
And giggling geriatrics stood upon their heads.
The gas in my dream, fell upon the USA,
Where people were waking up to yet another day
Of mugging, violence, gloom and threats of war
And wondering really was it really worth waking up for.
And then the happy gas spread throughout the land, And
all grew happy and yelled 'Ain't life grand?'

The mugger hugged his victim, dropped his gun.
They laughed together, together saw the fun,
The shops, the schools, the trains and all the places,
Were filled with merriment and such happy faces.
And to the Kremlin, the Heavenly gas drifted,
And instantly the Iron Curtain lifted.
And round the world for miles and miles and miles,
Humanity was rolling in the aisles.
Prime Ministers and Presidents gurgled 'Let's be friends
No more talks and treaties, now let's make amends.
Let's just be friendly, come now, make it snappy,
Hooray! the world's gone mad, we feel so happy.'
And then - I woke up. . .!

TURQUOISE

Turquoise is my favourite colour
Turquoise is a wonderful hue.
Seen in many variations,
Bluey green and greeny blue

Blue is the colour of peace and healing,
Green of loving, Nature, Spring.
Put the two of them together,
You have the best of everything.

Watch the colour of the sea,
The sparkle of an aquamarine,
The gleaming flash of a kingfisher,
A glimpse of emerald and opal seen.

CRYSTALS

Yes, maybe to you, they are stones,
Or gems to be bought and bartered,
And worn on hand and throat.
But to me, they are shining orbs,
Condensed energy of aeons and ages,
Translucent and glowing,
Vibrating.

Each is an individual
With its own power and life.
Patterned, coloured and shaped
Through time
By a Celestial hand
For us to use.
Hopefully for good.

THE DREAM

I dreamed and I dreamed, as all girls do
Of a shining knight on a white horse,
And I waited and waited my whole life through
'He won't come' they said, of course.

But fairy tales do come true, you know
For each one whose heart has yearned.
Yes, I kissed my frog, and like a miracle,
Into a Prince he turned.

SPRING

I'm looking forward
To the Spring
For the Spring to come again
To admire the golden daffodils
And feel the gentle, soothing rain.

To the Cherry Tree's glorious pink blossom
And the blackbird's sweet refrain
To the fresh new buds and green leaves
To Earth's wakening again

I'm looking forward to sunshine
To rainbows in the sky
To seeing my weeping willow
In green splendour reaching high

To watching all the parent birds
As they build nests for young
And each and every morning
Their joyful song is sung

To watch the joyful miracle
Of flowers come forth to bloom
In yellow, pink and blue and white
Oh, spring can't come too soon.

So Earth will soon awaken
From Winter's cold bitter grasp
The ice will melt, our hearts will lift
Spring come again at last.

FISH AND CHIPS

The Italians love pasta, the Frenchman his wine,
Paella for the Spanish, for the Chinese chow mein,
The Greeks love mousaka, the American his steak,
The Austrian, wiener schnitzel, the Belgian - cream cake.

The Indian loves curry, the Russian, borsht and sour cream,
The Hungarian loves goulash and Swiss fondues a dream.
But despite the invasion of many a new dish,
We still have the best one, fish and chips, chips and fish.

Fish and chips, fish and chips, fish and chips, fish and chips
It tastes so delicious, makes us all lick our lips.
There's plaice and there's haddock, there's cod and
                                        there's skate,
Shake the salt and the vinegar, please pile chips on my plate.

Wherever you wander, at work or at play,
The friendly fish and chip shop, never is far away.
The smell is so powerful, it can drift on for miles,
The effect is dramatic, changes frowns into smiles.
Just look at the face of someone eating a chip,
They're experiencing heaven, without taking the trip.

Fish and chips, fish and chips, fish and chips, fish and chips
It tastes so delicious, makes us all lick our lips.
There's plaice and there's haddock there's cod and
                                        there's skate,
Shake the salt and the vinegar, please pile chips on my plate.

QUIRKS

Yes, we may be a little *quirky*
Whatever the term may mean,
But we really feel quite perky
And fairly on the beam.

Well, I've looked for a definition
In the dictionaries I possess,
From the *Oxford* to the *Webster,*
And really, I must confess,

That looking all around me
At civilisations we have had,
I wonder just what is *normal*
And who or what is *mad.*

Now what about Madonna,
Michael Jackson and others such
Botham and Gazza, Thatcher and Bush
Come on now. Have they no quirks? - Not much!

Prince Charles, he talks to flowers,
The Queen to her corgis,
And are there any politicians
Free from quirky orgies?

We all have our little quirky ways,
And really it's quite fine,
It's what makes us all so human So unique and
so *divine.*

Yes, from the Greeks, to the Africans,
The Indians and the Turks,
Just about everyone
Has their *quirks!*

So what's yours?

GUILT?

The heavens won't fall,
If I don't wash the hall.
And if I don't dust,
The living room won't rust.

And who the hell cares
If I don't brush the stairs?
And friends won't forsake,
If the beds I don't make.

I'm not on the primrose path,
If I don't clean the bath.
Gabriel won't blow his horn,
If I don't mow the lawn.

Will God refuse me Heaven
If I don't get up at seven?
And will my neighbour think me obscene: If
my doorstep I don't clean?

A baby won't be less happy,
If I don't iron each nappy.
And my husband won't throw rocks,
If I forget to wash his socks.

If I don't Hoover the rugs,
We'll not be infested with bugs,
And if I don't make dinner today
There's always a Chinese take away.

AN ELIZABETHAN SONNET TO MY OPEN UNIVERSITY TUTOR

How does my time in trivia lie wasted,
When Art's wide vision beckons me anon.
In meagre hours from womb to tomb we hasteth,
Yet with the Muses, I would fair be gone.
But kin and household cares I first attendeth,
When to an essay I must needs aspire.
In drudgery my energy I spendeth,
Yet must I pen my tutor words of fire.
This *Mutability* - what doth it meaneth?
From units dim, dark depths, poor wits must
gleaneth. . .
O Shakespeare, Spencer, Daniel Southwold,
Greville,
Thy beauteous sonnets are the very devil.
If this means ought to you, dear reader, pray
Perchance the Gods will grant but once an °A'.

THOUGHTS

It's no good being too sensitive,
In this world that we live in.
No, you can't get very far,
If you've got too thin a skin.

Yes, it's best to be a tough guy,
And not to care a jot,
Whatever people think of you,
Whether nice or not.

ENGLISH SUMMER

Blackbirds trilling in the trees,
Sparrows chirping merrily,
Policemen showing off their knees,
This is summer!

Bees humming softly in the flowers,
Butterflies hovering for hours,
Windows wide open - you can hear the rows!
This is summer.

Ice cream consumed by the ton,
Sunshine enjoyed by everyone,
Life is easier - much more fun.
This is summer.

Rain and thunderstorms galore,
Umbrellas and raincoats are the more,
Cold winds bring sweaters to the fore,
This is summer"

ALLERGY

Allergy, allergy
What have you done to me?
I can't eat bread
I can't eat cake
And I can't eat the apple strudel
That I do love to make!

TEA

Our British Constitution
No longer may be glorious and free,
But the one heritage which will never fade
Is a lovely cup of tea.

We may have lots of worries,
And at times, tired we well may be,
But the world looks so much brighter
With a lovely cup of tea.

Whether the weather be hot or cold,
Whether on land or sea,
At four o'clock and indeed every hour,
We drink a cup of tea.

If you have a headache, cold or flu,
Or even housemaid's knee,
There's no better cure in the whole, wide
world,
Than a lovely cup of tea.

It's fine in mugs, in a glass, in jugs,
And in china of great delicacy.
You can slurp it, gulp it, tipple it, sip it,
It's still a cup of tea.

Some like it white, some like it black,
There's no apartheid rules you see
It makes the whole world into one
Does a lovely cup of tea.

Darjeeling, Earl Grey, Jasmine, and Ceylon,
There's tremendous variety
Whichever you choose, you will enjoy
Your lovely cup of tea.

Some like their tea with sugar,
And some honey from the bee,
Let's lift our cups in unison
And toast the cup of tea.

THE THINGS THEY DO

They put horses in stables.
Sardines in a tin.
And people in aeroplanes,
As if they're all thin.

No room for arms,
And no room for long legs.
Trapped in our seats
Like brandy in kegs.

A walk to the loo,
Becomes a sweet pleasure,
And the ability to breathe
Is a rare treasure.

COMPUTERS

I guess I'm computer illiterate
Don't understand the language at all
When the talk is of 'Windows' and software and such
I really could climb up the wall

It's true I've been given three lessons
And I'm now quite good at Solitaire
But I'm still not sure what keys to press
Just why, or how, or where

To talk to a true computer freak
You really mustn't dare
For they are in another world
That you somehow cannot share

It is as if they have been got at
By some strange, alien forces
Who have scrambled all their brain waves
And collected their resources

I admit that on a computer
A letter can be written so fine
But I can write a dozen letters
By hand in half the time!

THE COMMON COLD

Man has invented the car and the plane
The phone, radio and TV.
Man is the greatest,
So we've been told,
But - he still can't cure,
The common cold.

Man has conquered the mountains and seas,
Has flown to the moon and back,
He's adventurous, daring,
Brave and bold
But he still can't cure
The common cold.

So we take to our beds
And we splutter and sneeze,
Drink hot lemon and do as we're told
And we hope and pray
That perhaps one day
They will cure the common cold.

ANSWERPHONE

O answerphone
O answerphone
When I get through
It's always you!

I hear your voice
But you're not there
It fills me full
Of deep despair

I hear your message
And then the pip
I'd like to tear
You off a strip!

So are you there
Or are you not
Are you avoiding me
Or who or what?

O answerphone
O answerphone
When I get through
It's always you!

JUST LISTEN

Just listen to your heart
And it will tell you true
For all the answers that you need
Will be always there for you.

JUST BE

Just be
Just be a
Human being
No need to question
Why you are on this earth
No need to justify
That you were given birth
Just be.

IMP

There is a naughty imp
That chatters all day at me
He really drives me crazy And
never lets me be.

He says 'do this, do that, go here
Try this, try that, go there
Don't sit still, you must be busy'
Until my head is feeling dizzy.

He scoffs and scorns and smirks and snubs
At all I do and say
He negates and doubts and ridicules'
In every kind of way.

He's right there when I play or work
And when I drink and eat
And when I go to bed at night
I still hear his constant bleat.

And as soon as I'm awake again
He's with me right away
Ready with his chatter, chatter, chatter,
For yet another day.

If I choose to listen and obey
My peace he will destroy
So I must tune into my heart within
To feel that calm and joy.

CHILDREN'S SONG

God loves comedy,
That I know,
And if you don't believe me,
Just watch the passing show.

The funny little monkeys,
Swinging in the trees.
Wobbly, waddling ducks,
Babies' dimpled knees.

Puppies chasing tails,
And squealing piglets pink,
Fishes in the water,
Thirsty for a drink.

Spiny backed hedgehogs,
With black noses and shiny eyes.
Giraffes with long eyelashes,
And necks that reach so high.

Big old hippos,
Playing in the mud.
Bees collecting honey,
Cows calmly chewing cud.

So God loves comedy,
That I know,
And if you don't believe me,
Just watch the passing show.

NO!

When will I learn to say
No, no, no, no!
When someone cries 'Help!'
I get up and go.

'I need you!' they say
With despair on their face
But I need me *too*
And I need my own space.

I'll help all I can
But you must see
That I haven't got
Infinite energy.

I have things to do
And I need time to grow
So please don't be upset
If I have to say 'No°

ART CRITICS

'The Emperor thought
He was wearing fine clothes
When a little child knew
He wasn't wearing any.
You can fool some of the people
Some of the time
But in the end, you can't fool many.°

LAS VEGAS

So you finally got to Las Vegas
And saw the famous strip
Well don't you think it was divine?
No, frankly it gave me the pip!

Thousands of people playing machines
It was really more like a zoo
Except that all the animals there
Are quieter and more dignified too!

People look up at the bright lights
With gasps and OOOhs and aaahs!
But no-one notices the wonder
And miracle of the moon and the stars.

They come to spend and hope to win
And find their heaven as well
But from what I can see, now I've been there
It's how I imagine Hell!

JINGLE FOR LIVING

The best way to live,
Is one day at a time,
The present, not future or past.
All we have is right now,
Each moment is precious,
Time's passing, nothing will last.

There's remorse for the past,
For the future there's fear,
But what of the *now* that's today?
So joyfully savour it,
Enjoy the full flavour of it,
And you'll be living the best way.

MODERN 'ART°

Where has all the beauty gone
The art treasures that I love and know,
The Renoirs and the Monets,
Cezannes, Gaugins, Van Goghs?

The Art Galleries of the world now,
Are filled with such, mad ugly stuff,
Expressions of a sickly mind,
It's time we said en masse *'Enough!'*

ONLY A FILM

Last night I watched Paul Newman as a cop,
Who lived in New York, in the Bronx, the USA,
Watched his dilemma as he did his job,
The hate and the horrors he faced every day.

The place was filled with pushers, prostitutes and pimps,
 And thugs and thieves, and people high on drugs,
Dying from heroin, knives and gun shot wounds,
People hungry, angry, beset with filth and bugs.

It was sheer horror as I watched TV.
I thought is this the world we now live in,
Where a human life is less than drugs or gold,
Men born, die, and struggle in a rubbish bin?'

It was Dante's Inferno, Satan's Hell
Did God create this state? We know darn well,
That man has made a right mess in his way
Yes, we *crowns of creation* have gone a bit astray.

But wait - there's hope! Yes, I know it was a film
But -Paul Newman chose his conscience not his friend.
There was courage shown, love and humour too.
Goodness and Truth will win always in the end.

MRS TULLY

Dear Mrs Tully's, the salt of the earth.
A pearl beyond price is her true worth.
Every Monday and Thursday she cleans my house,
Good natured and honest and quiet as a mouse.
It's downstairs on Monday to see the week in,
And Thursday it's upstairs, all neat as a pin.
She first eats her sandwich, soup, fruit and Kit Kat,
And always has time for a nice little chat,
About her nineteen grandchildren, her children ten,
And all that they're doing, just where and just when.
She can make lovely clothes, her fingers are nimble.
Yes, she's so very clever with needle and thimble.
She's a great cook too, and you should just try
At Christmas, her puddings, Yule logs and mincepies.
And with marzipan and icing she can make,
A beautifully decorated wedding cake.

POLITICS

These political shenanigans
Are really quite a scream,
Men jostling for power,
To realise their dream.

Ashdown and Blair and Major,
Leaders as they may be,
Let's put them in a tiny boat,
And send them out to sea.

They can argue then amongst themselves,
And talk about their wishes,
Sort out their different policies,
And tell it to the fishes.

If they could put the people first,
And the country in which they thrive,
And, last of all, their party
We could get on with our lives.

FREEDOM

I'm learning to dance
To the rhythm of life
To soar like a bird
Set free,

To sway and to sing
Like a tree in the wind
I'm learning to be
Just me.

PART THREE

LOVE

To the one who has loved me always

and who I will always love.

TO RACHAEL (NEWLY BORN)

I love
Your dear little nose
And I love
Those delightful toes

I love
Those feet, those knees
And I even love it
When you sneeze

I love
That face of charm
Those fingers clasping mine
Those elbows and sweet arms

I love
The way you look at me
And seem to understand
All that you see

I love
The way you listen to me speak
I love
The little gurgles and the squeaks

I love
Those ears, that mouth
That dark fine hair
I wouldn't change you beautiful Rachael

For any other child
On Earth anywhere.

SHARON - 1

When you were born, I felt such joy - a little girl

The sweetest gift from God - a perfect pearl.

A child of beauty, joy and grace,

A radiant and charming baby face.

Your shining dark eyes were like jewels to see

More precious than diamonds you are to me.

From lovely child, to beautiful woman you grew,

Be happy always and to your own sweet self be true.

SHARON-2

Some time ago (seems only yesterday!)
God gave us a wonderful treasure
Not diamonds, rubies, silver or gold
But a more precious gift beyond measure.

Born in the sunshine of July
In royal Leo's sign
You are kind and generous and beautiful
Special, caring and fine.

DAVID

You were my firstborn, and at your birth
I was so happy to be on this earth.
You looked at me, as if to say
'Hello' - I knew we'd meet again some day.
And even then, your looks, intelligence and charms
Were evident as I held you in my arms,
I loved you, oh so much, so special were you to me,
And you are special still, and you will always be.

MARTIN

From the very first, you were so good, so sweet
A happy baby - beautiful - from head to feet.
Brown hair, pink cheeks, and eyes deep blue
You were so big and bonny, straight and true.
A contented child right from the start.
So good to be with,
I loved you with all my heart.
You've grown tall and kind and loved by all
Warm and loving to everyone, both big and small.

MOTHER

I carried you,
And gave you birth,
So you could live,
This life on earth.

I heard you talk,
I dried your tears,
And saw you walk,
And calmed your fears.

Took you to school,
And watched you grow,
I'll love you always,
As well you know.

Now you are grown,
My work is through,
And now dear one,
It's up to you.

LET ME

O Let me see with the eyes of the heart
And not with the eyes of the mind,
To see the love in you and in me,
Not judge or be unkind.

O Let me hear with the ears of my heart,
And not with the ears of the mind,
To hear the sweet harmonies that are within,
Not the noise outside that we find.

O Let me feel with a heart that's true,
And not with my mind analyse,
To feel the peace and joy that's real,
Not unconsciously criticise.

O Let me touch the soft, gentle heart,
Not the hard callused rock of the mind,
The trust and gratitude, joy, and peace,
Can never be denied.

O Let me taste the sweetness of the heart,
Not the bitterness of the mind
Let me choose to listen to my heart always
And experience the divine.

LOVE

What is it in you that I love?
Is it your hair?
Once dark, now grey,
Is it your eyes?
Warm and kind,
But often tired and withdrawn.
Is it your voice?
Loving words, tender, sweet,
But sometimes critical and sharp,
Is it your touch?

No

That which I love in you
Is who you *really* are,
Which was, is, and ever shall be
Unchanging, eternal, immortal energy.
Who you *truly* are,
Truth, love, joy and consciousness.
Your heart speaking soundlessly to my heart,
Love seeing love,
Life feeling life,
God touching God.

YOU ARE

You are the sun that warms my heart
You are the wind that gives my breath.
You are the love that carries me,
On my brief journey from birth to death.

You are the rain that slakes my thirst,
You are the stars that wondrously shine,
You are the rainbow in the sky,
That shows me hope and joy are mine.

BEST FRIEND

Do you know how much I love you,
Will you ever realise?
Can't you hear it in my voice,
Can't you see it in my eyes?

I loved you from the very first,
Through all the years that have now passed,
I love you dearly every day,
I'll love you at the very last.

And when all else has let you down,
And even friends you hold so dear,
 Remember you are not alone,
For my dear one, I'll still be here.

To a new-born grandchild
LITTLE ONE

Little one,
Precious one,
Child of my child,
Welcome to this Earth

You have come
Trailing clouds of glory'
With innocence and joy
Wonder, love and purity.

Little miracle
Blissfully asleep
What potential is there
In that tiny form?

Little hands
So perfect
What will they do
As you grow?

Such sweetness
Such perfection
My heart sings
As I look at you.

As I hold you
In my arms
I feel such joy
And such fulfilment.

You have come
To adorn the world
To heal and to love
And to bring happiness

FEELINGS

Feelings too deep for words,
A love that is real and true,
How can I ever tell,
How very much I feel for you.

The radiance of a baby's smile,
The freshness of early morning dawn,
The fragrance of a flowering rose,
The blackbird's glorious song each morn.

The majesty of mountains far,
The cool, green shade of a willow tree,
The silvery moon, the starry skies,
Manifest the wonder of you to me.

WHAT IS LOVE?

Love is tenderness
Love is patience
Love is gentleness
Love is tolerance
Love is kindness
Love is mindfulness of others
Love is appreciation
Love is helping others
Love is gratitude
Love given, comes back always
Love flows
Love is joy.

AU REVOIR

Au revoir my dear one
      °Til again we meet,
The deep love that I feel
      Made parting, bitter-sweet.

I do not know,
      When we will meet again,
But spring comes after winter,
      And sunshine follows rain.

The world keeps on turning,
      And day and night go by
The birds will keep on singing
      While stars shine in the sky.

Yes, truly, time makes changes,
      We will not be the same,
But I know the love we shared,
      Will always stay aflame.

TOGETHER

Together
We can ride the storm,
Until peace and joy again
Become the norm.

Together
We can be real,
Ignore the *ought* and *musts*
Do what we feel.

Together
We can be true,
Forget the past that's gone
Embrace what's new.

Together
We can live each day,
Not fret about tomorrow
Come what may.

PRIZEWINNER

'I never win anything' you said
'But you have won *everything*'
I replied 'You've won a life and many days,
Been given breath, a time to play,
The world is yours and all that's in it
While you are here, so just join in it
Enjoy your prize, it is the best
Better than money and all the rest.'

YOU AND I

We can be happy you and I,
No matter what the world can do,
Together can feel happiness,
For you have me and I have you.

We can be happy you and I,
And every day can start anew,
With hope and love within our hearts,
For you have me and I have you.

We can be happy you and I,
We have a love that's tried and true,
And really all that matters is,
That you love me and I love you.

YOUNG MOTHERS

Young mothers
With their first child
So beautiful, so tender
 Looking sweetly
At their baby
Protecting
And surrounding them
With a circle of love.

SUNRISE

This morning I rose early
To see the gold sun rise
As the blanket of darkness lifted
Colour flooded through the skies

A wash of orange, pink and red
Began suffusing to my view
And as I looked at this awesome sight
I saw mauve, indigo and blue

It was so quiet and peaceful
Through the air the birds flew silent and free
The trees stood still as sentinels
A daily miracle to see

ANNIVERSARY SONG

I feel very blessed
That you chose me,
To live together
In matrimony.

I see we were meant
To be together,
To learn so much
From one another. (Despite some stormy *weather).*

I feel very blessed
That you are there,
To give me a smile
To show that you care.

A touch, a hug,
A special look.
You won't find that
In a *Mills and Boon* book.

KNOWING

It's not that I believe,
But that I *know,*
It's not because someone else,
Has told me so.

It's not a fantasy,
It's what I feel,
It is truth ultimate,
It alone is real.

The force of life
Within you and me,
Is in every living form,
Man, bird, fish, flower, tree.

And if you can tune in
To this miracle on Earth,
You too will understand,
Why you were given birth.

THE LORD IS MY SHEPHERD

The Lord is my shepherd
I am His lamb
He loves me exactly
As I am.

LOTUS

On this wonderful Earth
On which we are living
There is so much beauty
That has been given

Everthing in this world
Be it bird, animal or tree
Is not only beautiful
But teaches you, teaches me

The immaculate lotus
With flowers pink and white,
Is there to appreciate
And for us to delight

It teaches a lesson
When we are aware
It roots are in dirty water
But the flowers rise to the air

Never does the flower touch
Though the water may rise higher
It keeps its purity
To emulate and admire.

DAD

You loved beautiful things
The roses in your garden
Music - I saw you cry
When you heard music that moved you
You loved antiques, and often brought home
Some lovely old things you had found in a shop
I remember the tall Grandfather clock in the hall
You would wind it up every Sunday
With a big gold key.

You had silver hair brushed back
And a silver moustache that tickled
When you kissed me
And a deep, warm voice
Twinkly blue eyes,
Your charm and Russian accent
Never left you
I remember your Sunday cigar
An aroma that permeated the house.

How hard you worked
And how little leisure
And so little time
I miss you.
You gave me so much,
I felt safe, protected,
And, yes, I love beautiful things too,
And music, and roses,
And I remember you with love and gratitude.

ROSE

I hardly knew you,
I was only eleven
When you left this world.
I remember only a sweetness.

You gave me chocolates,
And you had a cough,
And went to hospital,
And you never came home.

I remember your brown and white check jacket,
And I have a photograph,
But I sense a sweet presence
Around me sometimes
And I know you are there still.

Let me be a rose
Growing in your garden
Radiating sweet perfume
Of your love.

IF

If we could but realise
That everything is fine
For we all have a direct line
To the Divine.

WHEN WE HAVE EARS TO HEAR

When we have the ears to hear
And the eyes to see
Only then can we experience
True reality.

Flowers and jewels
Of glowing hue
Are as naught to what is
Within me and you.

The sweet song of birds
On the wing or in trees
Are but a shadow
Of inner harmonies.

RESURRECTION

I feel like a delicate flower
Trying to grow
To lift my head
Above the ground

Yet I am buffeted
By the cruel words
Trodden down by rough feet
Hurt by noise, cruelty, pollution

Yet the tiny snowdrop
Though so fragile and frail
In the cold, dark winter
Against all odds

Breaks through the hard, icy, earth
To grow and bloom and raise her graceful
head
For us to enjoy, to marvel, to hope
For Spring --- a resurrection

LET ME BE

Lord, let me be loving Lord
let me be true So I can be
Of good use to you.

Let me be merry
Let me be strong
So I can laugh
At the things that go wrong.

Let me be patient
Let me be still
So I can hear your voice And
know your will.

THANK YOU

I thank you
For giving me this time
To live, to love, to learn, to be,
To savour each breath
Each precious moment
And to enjoy still, being me.

To see the trees
Lifting to the sky
The birds soaring
Up above,
The beauty of this life on Earth
To see in all, Your care and love.

MY HEART SINGS

How is it that my heart sings,
When Winter is grey and dark.
The earth is cold, the birds are still,
And the trees stand bare and stark.

Why is it that my heart sings?
The Media is full of gloom.
Men hasten through violence, war and disease,
To what seems an inevitable doom.

How can I feel joy and love in my heart
With so much grief, pain and strife?
Men unconscious of their precious gift
The miracle of human life.

Why do I feel gladness in my heart?
It was given us at our birth,
By the One who with infinite tenderness,
Brought us to this beautiful earth.

We can all feel that song that our hearts sing,
It will truly make us free,
For the joy and the love that we feel in our heart,
Is our true immortality.

DUTY

'Do what you ought' the preacher said.
 'Do your *duty* always, not what you feel.'
I've done that all my whole life through
Been *nice* and *done good* *'til* it felt unreal.

So what is this feeling that is inside?
As deep within it smiles and sighs,
That cries to me 'I am denied!
Follow the truth that within you lies!'

'You have a choice' the preacher said
Of being Christian, Moslem, Buddhist, Jew.'
But what are we at birth and death
Does religion, nationality, count then to you?

A human being is what I wish to be
Realising the one true God who put me here,
Experiencing the love He has for me.
He is not a God of guilt or fear.

So follow your heart, and not your mind
Or your emotions or impulses that can control.
Follow the truth within yourself
It is your true being, it is your soul.

ANNIVERSARY

It's our Anniversary
Another year
So swiftly flown by
Where do they all go?
Days spent together
Sharing our time
Living together
Growing together
Loving together
Experiencing together
Many, many things;
Joys and sorrows
Delights and disappointments
Not always seeing eye to eye
For we are individuals
Yet happy to be together still
And still in love
And loving each other
It's our Anniversary
God willing, we'll have more
Happy Anniversary.

WHAT WILL YOU DO?

So what will you do
With the rest of your life?
I'll enjoy myself, that's what!
I'll do all the things that I love to do,
And ignore those 'shoulds° and °must not

I won't allow anyone to stress me out
Or order me about
If I'm depressed sometimes, well I'll get over it
If I'm angry then I'll jolly well shout.

I'll not bottle up my feelings anymore
To be thought of as nice and such a gentle soul.
No, I'll be myself, even if unpopular.
To be true to myself is my new role.

I'll enjoy each moment of each day
Like a child whose eyes are brand new.
See each leaf and flower, birds and clouds in the sky
With wonder and with awareness I will view!

I'll sit under the Willow in the summer time,
And feel the sunshine filtering through.
Hear the thrilling song of the blackbirds,
And enjoy the flowers' perfume and hue.

I'll meditate and write and I'll paint and I'll walk, And
stroke my lovely white cat, Listen to Mozart, Vivaldi
and Bach So what will I do? That is that!

TOMORROW'S HOPE

The children of today
And God's gift for tomorrow
Through them a Golden Age of Love
And Joy, will banish sorrow

They herald a time of peace and hope
And light for all to see
It is not an empty dream
But what is meant to be

A true brotherhood of man
Will manifest on this Earth
And no child will suffer hunger
Because of humble birth

All races, religions and nations
Will live in true harmony
With respect and love for all of life
God's plan for humanity.

TRUE HOME

This body
Is like a hotel room,
Lived in temporarily,
In relative comfort.
Sometimes things go wrong,
The taps don't turn on properly
It's not easy to sleep,
The air conditioning doesn't work,
And it never really belongs to you,
For you eventually have to give back the key.

This heart, this soul
Is our true home.
No harm can befall it,
No discomfort touch it,
It's never too hot or too cold.
Always the right temperature,
Always peaceful, always calm.
No problems in our true home,
Where we live in blissful comfort,
And --- we get to keep the key forever!

DOUBTS

I've had my doubts, I've had my fears
I've had them many, many years,
Dwelt in the past, and took the blame,
I felt unworthy, full of shame.

The future too, became for me
A mist of negativity,
Until you came and made me see,
It was alright to just be me.

There was no bad, there was no good,
There was no -*you mustn't! You're wrong! You should!*
I could relax, there was no sin,
And Heaven could be found within.

You showed me love,
You set me free,
I am so grateful,
That you found me.

PATIENCE

We are not born with patience
A baby can not wait for food
For milk, for changing, for cuddles
You can't say 'be patient' to a baby
He wants it now
He wants his needs met <u>now</u>

And a toddler has no patience either
If he wants your attention
Or a toy that attracts him
He wants it now
Or he may scream and have tantrums
You can't tell him to be patient.

But when we get to school
We are forced to begin to learn patience
There are others to be considered
And you have to take your turn
It's not easy and we become frustrated
And maybe a little resentful and angry.

Later, with life experience we may learn
The true meaning of patience
Which is surrender and courage, caring and love
for others and ourselves
And serenity and gentleness and humility
And faith and trust that all will be well
And there is a time for everything.

THE BOOKS THAT I READ

The books that I read,
The people I meet,
The music I hear,
Are God speaking to me.

The air that I breathe,
The water I drink,
The food that I eat,
Are God's Grace to me.

The smile of a child,
The touch of a friend,
The lick of a dog,
Are God loving me.

Whatever I do,
Wherever I go,
Whatever is said,
God's there for me.

In the song of a bird,
The fall of a leaf,
The smell of a flower,
God manifests to me.

YOU MUST!

You must do this
You must do that
Or what will people think!
You must go here
You must go there
To keep you in the pink.

Don't ask so many questions
It's part of a tradition
You have to do (what we think) right
Conform to your condition.

But I really wasn't born a sheep
I'm a free human being
I don't wish to follow blindly
But be conscious of what I'm seeing.

So I will follow my own heart
And do what I feel is right
And be honest to my own true self
And thus to others with all my might.

THE POTTER'S WHEEL

Shaped and moulded on the Potter's wheel,
Seemingly indifferent to the pain you feel.
Dross and ego burned in the kiln's fire,
Attachments, anger and desire.

Intensive heat as if of Hell's glow,
Confusion, fear, and nowhere to go.
No-one to help, no-one to trust,
All hopes and longings turned to dust.

But from the Potter's loving hands
A pure gold vessel - glowing - stands,
Stripped of all grosser ornament,
Now ready for use as His instrument.

LOVE

My love for you
Grows through the years.
My life you've filled
With joy, not tears.

A life of love
So true, so free,
I'm so grateful
You revealed to me -

The beauty
That within I find,
The magic
And the peace of mind.

I love you more
As time goes by,
You taught my heart
To sing and fly.

How can I express
My thanks to you?
I'll love you all
My whole life through.

THIS TIME LET IT BE

Deep in my heart, my soul, my being
I know you,
As I have always known,
Through ageless ages, from the beginning of time.
Your voice, your face, your smile,
There for me.

Time after time, life after life,
You came,
With endless love and patience and forgiveness,
To help me, to show me, to guide me:
A hesitant step I took, another, and then held back.
Fearful, untrusting and full of doubt.

You have come again and so have I.
This time, let it be
All the way,
Step after step, my hand held in yours,
With trust and humility, love and devotion,
Committed to the path.

With hope and with courage,
With joy and with love,
This time, let it be.
My hand in yours, yours in mine,
All the way to the end and to the beginning
My guide, my teacher, my friend.

I SEE YOUR LOVE

'Thou shalt love the Lord they God with all thy heart
and with all thy soul and with all thy might'

It seemed so hard to love you Lord
When I couldn't touch you, hear you, or see.
But now the most wonderful secret
My heart has revealed to me.
When I try to love all your creatures,
And love myself and all that I do,
I see that in reality
I'll then truly be loving you.

I see your smile
In the smile of every child,
Your tender tears
In every drop of rain.
I see your laughter
In Autumn's dancing leaves,
Your tenderness
For all in pain.

I see your love,
In every face
And in the eyes
Of everyone I know.
I see your hope,
In every new born babe.
I feel the faith and trust
In you, within me grow.

I feel your love,
In every flower, every tree.
In birds, fish, animals
And every living thing.
At sunrise, sunset,
In stars, sea, moon
And mountains high,
I see You, manifest, in everything.

IT IS ENOUGH

It is enough,
To be here now.
To learn, to love, To know.

It is enough,
To have this time,
To feel, and let
This heart - so precious - grow.

No need for riches, travel or acclaim,
We have it all,
Can feel that joy,
For we have breathed that name.

It is enough!

I HAVE SEEN

I have seen
The sun rise and set In all its glory.

I have seen
Stars in the Southern skies
Sparkling like jewels.

I have seen
Gentle rain and rainbows
And dew, and felt soft winds.

I have seen
Flowers pierce through the earth
And fill the world with colour and fragrance.

I have seen
The sea in its magnificence
Rolling into the shore.

I have seen
Birds flying high
And heard their joyous songs.

I have seen
The pride and dignity of animals
And loved their sweetness.

I have seen
The love in eyes of men
And seen the beauty shining through.

I have seen
Awesome mountains, lakes and rivers
And marvelled at Nature's work.

I have seen
That radiant face and heard those words
And felt that love.

WHY?

Why God why
Why God, why me?
What kind of karma do I have
That this has to be?

Then again ---

Why God why
Why not me
For none of us are immune
From the ills of humanity.

DON'T LOVE SO MUCH

'Don't love so much, don't love so much,' you say
So can you tell a child it cannot play?
Or stop the mighty ocean's ebb and flow
Or tell a flower that it must not grow?

'Don't love so much, don't love so much,' you plead
Oh but I have to love, it is my need
Just as we need to breathe, to drink, to eat
To feel the sun's rays, grass beneath our feet
The moon is meant to shine, the stars to glow
And we are born to love, as deep within we know.

'Don't love so much, don't love so much,' you cry
Yes, love can hurt so much, we almost die
But would you want me to hate, spurn, or to ignore,
Or live unwanted, lonely, lost for ever more?

Yes, 'Don't love so much, don't love so much,
                                        you said
But I will keep on loving 'til I'm dead
And even then, by God's eternal Grace
I'll love you still, another time, another place.

SEPTEMBER

It was so glorious to see you It seems
such a long, long while,
Since I heard your loving voice
And saw your gorgeous smile.

I hope I can always remember
The wise words that you said,
On those sweet days in September
With my heart and with my head.

You said, °Appreciate this miraculous Earth
And the joyous beauties we see,
The vast sky with its myriad stars
Every dancing leaf on each tree.

Appreciate this gift of life
Focus on joy, love, peace and good,
Know yourself, accept and be happy
As much as you know you should.'

TOUCH

Touch is our God given sense
Of love and care,
A gentle touch Is like a prayer.

The energy channelled through
From one to another,
To show that
You are my sister, my brother.

A kiss, a hug,
Express what we feel,
And a kind hand on a shoulder,
Can only heal.

Without a loving touch,
A child cannot thrive,
And someone seldom touched,
Is only half alive.

A caring touch
Shows love and feeling,
Surely then we should use
God's gift for healing.

CELEBRATION

Join in the celebration.
Enjoy the beauty,
And experience the joy,
And appreciate the gift,
Of this precious thing
Called Life!

Join in the celebration.
Dance with the music,
And sing to the melody,
And sway to the rhythm,
Of this precious gift
Called Life!

Join in the celebration.
See the shining colours,
And the light and the glory,
And the radiant rainbow,
Of this precious gift
Called Life!

Join in the celebration
Breathe in the perfume,
And taste the sweetness,
Be here and now,
With this precious gift
Called Life!

YOU ARE THE ONE

You are the one,
Who showed us
What life really means.
You are the one,
Whose love mends
All our shattered dreams.

You are the one,
Awakening us to
This wondrous earth.
You are the one,
Showing us the gift
We received at birth.

You are the one,
Whose faith in us
We deeply feel,
You are the one,
In whose love and care
Our hearts can heal.

You are the one!

LOVES

I love Beethoven, Mozart and Bach,
 I love walking in the park.
I love stroking cats, to hear them purr,
I love patting a dog's hairy fur.
I love bananas, apples and cherries,
Ripe pears, peaches and strawberries.
I love someone massaging my feet.
I love dancing to a Latin beat.

I love old movies, comedies are best.
Cary Grant, Gary Cooper, Clark Gable and the rest.
I love babies' gurgles and their bright eyes.
I love Christmas pudding and I love mincepies.
I love wallowing in a hot bath.
I love log fires on an open hearth.
I love the thrill of blackbirds' singing.
I love to hear those church bells ringing.

I love the smell of a red rose after rain.
I love the sound of a distant train.
I love the countryside, cows, horses, sheep.
I'd love to get a good night's sleep!
I would love to see a butterfly
And to hear an owl's distant cry.
I love the shade of a willow tree.
I love you and you love me.

PART FOUR

NATURE
AND
ANIMALS

°Nature never did betray - the heart that loved her.'
William Wordsworth

'Animals are such agreeable friends,
they ask no questions, they pass no criticisms.'
George Elliot

RUFUS

'He was only a dog,' you say.
But, he was my friend, my dear, dear friend.
He shared my day and night, my food, my bed, my
life.
I held his soft paw and talked to him for comfort,
When I cannot so hold your hand and talk to you.
When I was ill, he would not leave my side
But, people quickly leave and go about their work.

'He was only a dog,' you say.
How ignorant, how arrogant!
Did not the same life force beat in him as in you?
Did not God breathe him as He breathes you or me?
The Creator made every hair and pad with love and
care.
Those brown eyes looked out with life and love.
He did the best he could,
Imprisoned in a body that could not realise God,
Until He took pity and rescued him.

'He was only a dog,' you say.
But the lessons I learned from him!
Of joy and laughter, of play, and just to *be!*
The lesson of never wavering devotion,
Of longing to be with his *master.*
The pain of separation, the joy of reunion,
Every atom of his being directed to love.
I never can forget.
Thank you Lord for the gift you gave me.

ANIMALS

I love animals.
I love their simplicity,
And their naturalness,
Their trust and their love.

They are not devious,
They do not prevaricate
They just are
Themselves.

I love to touch them,
The silky softness of
A cat's fur
A dog's hairy coat.

I love the love in their eyes
The sweetness,
The innocence
They don't hide anything.

I love the way they move,
The grace, the suppleness,
The agility
Just watch a cat, dog, a horse.

I love their playfulness
Their joy in being alive,
They are like little children,
That never grow up.

I love to watch them.
They have no self-consciousness,
No pretence, no sophistication,
They just are.

POTSWORTH

There once was a Springer called Potsworth,
In Battersea Dogs' Home 'twas found,
And despite his one pet obsession
To me, he's the best dog around.

He's bright, and he's big, and he's bouncy,
He comes right away when I call,
But from morning to night, he's determined
To have you throw his favourite ball.

You throw it once and he catches,
And puts it right back on the floor.
You throw it again! And again!
And again! But like Oliver, he asks for more.

So after you've scored quite a century
Of throws and of catches - clever stuff!
You sink to your knees in exhaustion,
Gasping *'P o t s w o r t h!* - Enough is enough!'

POM POM

Dear faithful friend, we miss you so,
Those loving eyes no longer glow,
No wet, black nose and wagging tail
A welcome that would never fail.

No-one could have a better pal.
More constant, tolerant and loyal,
Who made the best of bad and good,
And understood my every mood.

A busy road, a moonless night,
In seconds you were gone from sight,
Cruel blow of fate, this way to bless.
A dog who gave such happiness.

Dear Lord, if man could only know
The qualities, animals to us show,
Then maybe since the world began,
We'd have a brotherhood of man

SEASONS

Spring is giggly, young and gay,
Summer is flowing and laughs every day.
Autumn is smiling as she matures,
But Winter is serious as the cold she endures.

UP WITH THE LARK

When the first bird twitters,
Even before it is light,
Chico the cat is up,
Ready and bright.

He jumps on my bed,
Though it's only daybreak,
And gently miaows,
To make sure I'm awake.

He's not very patient,
So if I don't stir,
He will put out a paw,
And gently pull at my hair.

MY FURRY FRIEND

My friend is furry.
And has a tail.
He's very handsome.
For a male.

We sit in summer
Beneath the willow.
At night he sleeps.
Upon my pillow.

SAFARI WITH SHEBA

There's a Safari at the bottom of my garden.
Yes, a lively wealth of wild life there abounds.
It's true there are no elephants, or hippos, or
                                        giraffes,
Or lions, or tigers prowling round the grounds.
But we do have a saucy squirrel in the oak tree,
And a snuffly hedgehog with black eyes and cute
                                        black nose,
And a field mouse scampers by on tiny feet,
And honey bees sip nectar from a rose.
There are butterflies fluttering round the Buddlea,
Red Admirals in force, and Cabbage Whites,
Black beetles march in order down the pathways,
On the bird table, two starlings start to fight.

There are Blackbirds singing sweetly in the willow,
Magpies chattering in the tall, green firs,
Sparrows squabble, Blue-tits balance on the
                                        peanuts,
And *that* Springer Spaniel has ears full of burrs.
Four cats walk blithely down the grassy lawn,
With suppleness and glossy fur and grace.
One is black and white with bright green eyes and
                                        chutzpah,
One a small black kitten with a thin sweet face.
The third is called *Minkie* and is handsome,
With thick cream coat and furry fluffy tail.
But the fourth cat is the one who *owns* the garden
And she's the *'beautifulest'* creature of them all.

THE ELEPHANT

The elephant is an awesome creature,
In any landscape, the biggest feature,
With impressive body, feet and head,
Yet soft and gentle is his tread.

He is an example to us all,
Loving to his fellows and loyal,
He does not kill for sport or pride,
But eats the leaves Nature provides.

I've looked an elephant in the eye,
And what I saw made me want to cry.
Such an innocence and sweetness there to see,
So simple, yet so great a creature is he.

UNICORN

O wondrous creature,
Did you really exist?
If so,
What a glorious sight
We have missed.
Such beauty, such grace and mystery.
A part of old world history.
A creature so pure, so noble, so free,
You *may* be a myth,
But you still live for me.

147

LITTLE CAT

A little cat
Sleeps upon my bed.
Pink nose, tender ears
Emerald eyes shut fast.

Head cradled in soft paws,
Bushy white tail
Tucked under neatly,
Lost in slumber.

A gentle purring,
Softly vibrating,
Peacefully, tranquilly
Sends me to sleep.

CONTRAST

So delicate,
Those soft white paws,
As he leaps
Gently on to my bed.

And yet those paws
Can catch a mouse,
And with teeth and claws,
Tear him limb from limb.

TO POTSWORTH

You may be a canine geriatric
Still I think you're a lovely creature,
In your garden or house or on our TV
You still are an outstanding feature.

You still bark a lot though you don't hear so well,
And you love playing still with a ball.
Yes, you still wag your tail and you love everyone,
But you love your Viv and Martin most of all

(and we love you too!)

CHICO -1

Abracadabra Silver Chico Chinchilla,
The Latin name of a rare caterpillar?
No, the true title of our little white cat,
We call *Chico,* or *Cheeky, Puss, Boy,* or what's that?

But we'll sing his praises for he's really a beaut,
Thick, silvery white fur and pink nose so cute,
With glowing eyes of sea-green and a look of disdain,
An aristocrat cat from his tail to his mane.

CHICO - 2

White cat, fluffy cat,
Cat that I adore,
Watching the rain teaming down
At the open door.

'Why can't you change the weather?'
Your emerald eyes implore.
'I need to play and run and prowl,
You've got the power I'm sure.°

White cat, fluffy cat.
See, here comes the sun.
Into the garden now you go.
Until the day is done.

THE SIMPLE LIFE

It's such a joy
To have an animal in the house
Whether cat or dog
Or hamster, rabbit, mouse.

They show us
Just how simple life can be
Instead of rushing around (as we do)
In perplexity.

BIRD IN THE WILLOW

Little bird, little bird,
Singing in the willow tree.
I know you sing for your territory.
Yet I feel you sing for me.

Your throat swells with your singing,
And vibrates with each note.
Every atom of your being,
Is poured out by your heart.

In the still pure air of morning,
Your voice rings out so clear.
So joyful and so beautiful
To rejoice our ears to hear.

Little bird, little bird,
Singing in the willow tree.
I feel you sing in gratitude
For the life given you so free.

O GIVE ME ANIMALS EVERY TIME

Oh give me animals every time.
They don't grumble, they don't judge, or lay down
                                    the law.
They don't shout, or argue, or push, or shove,
They just like you, and love you, and hold up a paw.
Oh give me animals every time.
They don't reject you, neglect you, nor do they bore,
Or make you feel sad or make you feel bad
And you can always put them outside the door.

SHEBA AND KITTEN

Sinuous, slinky, sensuous soul,
Such scenes those shining eyes have seen.
Wisdom of Solomon in your stare.
Fathomless shadows.
Dark-eyed queen.

Softly enfolded in padded paws,
Madonna look as your kitten drinks.
Patiently purring, as tender as Eve,
A moment of peace
In a world of noise.

SHEBA -1

My little cat, my loving friend has gone.
And how I miss her, none can ever know but I,
And now she sleeps forever in the garden that she
                                    roamed,
Where on the soft, green grass, she did so love to lie.
From her blue eyes, so much love showered on me.
She purred and licked me as I stroked her ears and
throat.
God's graceful creature, so loving, truly beautiful,
She was just pure love inside a furry coat.

SKYLARKS

Oh you skylarks, you birds of joy,
Singing and flying, high and higher in the sky,
Soaring and skimming, over the blue horizon,
Looking down at fields, and trees, and men.
What songs of praises to your Creator,
What notes of bliss, so pure, so sweet, so true.

Your song is like a flute played by a child.
Celestial musicians sent to give us hope,
To rouse our spirits from the dark, dense earth
And lift them to the skies,
To realms beyond this world of Ilusion,
To the beautiful reality of truth.

SUNFLOWER

I watched you grow
From a tiny seed
I was a witness
To your birth
I saw the fragile stem and leaves appear
That showed above the earth.

You grew so tall
You grew so strong
A miracle to see
Until you stood quite eight feet tall
Much taller by far
Than me.

In the garden every morning I would go
to visit you
And waited for your flowers Golden
yellow to come through

And now I've seen them open
In their full beauty to the sun
Your smiling happy faces
Bring joy to everyone.

THE WALK

We walked over the springy grass,
So alive, yet so yielding.
It surrendered to our feet,
Yet sprang up again as we passed,
Strong, crisp, and unharmed.
The sweet perfume of the cut grass,
And the tangy wood smoke,
Filled us with their fragrance.

I touched the laurel leaves, the chestnut tree,
The russet apples half grown, unripe,
Rested my hands against the ancient trees,
Felt the living energy, the flowing sap.
They are so awesome, so miraculous,
Branches lifted to the sky, defying gravity,
Abundant nature - multitudes of leaves,
Each tree unique, each leaf unlike another,
Each a living wonder of veins and sweet, green life.
We tuned in to the vibrating energy.

MUSIC

When I hear great music
I want to stretch out my arms
And embrace the whole world
And express my gratitude
For its glory and consolation

AUTUMN COLOUR

Russet and red
And all shades of green,
The rich leaves of autumn
Are a glory to be seen.

Orange and yellow,
And brown and gold,
The October trees
Are a joy to behold.

Beech, oak and maple,
Without a sound,
Drop their leaves gently
To the ground.

With shouts of glee,
And feet that crunch,
The leaves are trampled
With satisfying scrunch,

WATER

Flowing, pouring, rushing,
Streaming, glistening, falling,
Splashing, showering, puddling,
Refreshing, running, roaring,
Energising, cleansing, life giving
Water!

EARLY MORNING

Early morning;
The quiet time,
The best time.
No noise, no rush.
No cars, no people.
Only Chico and me.
The air fragrant and pure
So fresh and vital.

Birds start to sing.
A blackbird, a robin,
Doves cooing gently,
Dawn a rose pink glow
Sun just beginning to rise
For a new born day.
Rain softly falling
Trees swaying in the breeze.

I throw out the crumbs
And raisins, and nuts,
A pigeon swiftly swoops down
And two chattering magpies.
Three black crows strut the grass
Like stiff legged Gauleiters.
Blue-tits flit in and out,
A grey squirrel eats his fill.

It's a magical time.
The quiet time,
The best time,
Each morning a new day.
Each day a rebirth.
Each morning a miracle unfolds
Before my eyes,
And I can witness it!

CHERRY TREE

We gaze at each other
Through the kitchen window,
As we have looked
For three and thirty years.

You are always so beautiful
At every season,
In the spring, the buds appear again
So fresh, so tender, so green.

Then the pink delicate blossom,
Breathtakingly lovely,
Fairylike, unreal, fragile,
For such a short, sweet span.

You stay just for us to marvel,
Then your flowers begin to fall
Like soft confetti to the grass,
A wonderful carpet of pink.

Then your leaves in their green splendour,
Your branches a mass of green,
Flourish through the summer,
Giving shade and shelter to birds and to me.

Then one day, I see a red leaf
Then another and another and another,
Harbinger of Autumn, nostalgic sadness,
'Till all your leaves are red.

Now a magnificent fiery burning bush.
The winds come, the leaves fall
One by one, slowly at first
And then faster and faster blowing onto the
grass.

And finally your branches are held to the sky
As if in supplication
Bare, naked, simple and beautiful
Waiting, waiting for the touch of Spring.

OCTOBER MAGIC

We sat on the wooden bench
Amongst the gently swaying trees
Leaves --- yellow and brown and orange
A thick carpet for our feet
It was a magical moment
The late October sun shone warmly
Birds twittered sweetly
And a squirrel scampered by
Distant voices and the hum of traffic
The breeze stirred in the branches
And softly touched our hair
The grass smelled fresh and sweet
We sat and closed our eyes
And drank in the peace and calm of it
A few moments
A precious gem carved out of time.

AUGUST (MUSINGS)

In my garden its the last day of August, - sun shining intermittently -sky blue, lots of fluffy white clouds. A breeze is blowing, growing in crescendo to a soft wind - making the trees dance to its choreography. The weeping willow does a hula-hula dance, the silver birches daintily shake their leaves like a petite Chinese lady. The three tall, tall larches sway almost dangerously backwards and forwards, sideways and sideways, as if saying 'No, no, no!' (How do they stay up there?) - and the fir tree is replying 'Yes, yes, yes!'

The sun glistens the leaves so they appear like precious jewels - jade and emerald. It's warm, but there's a tang in the air of approaching Autumn, a sadness, a nostalgia for the departing summer.

Some birds sing quietly, but there are no dawn choruses, no great activity, no thrilling evening songs from blackbirds and thrushes -preparation for migration to warmer climes being made by some birds, and others, resting after the demands of mating, nest making and rearing of young.

This is the last day of August. Tomorrow is September. Meanwhile, I sit here in the garden. I am here, at this moment, in this garden, on this planet - on this Earth.

What did Keats say? °Truth is Beauty, Beauty, Truth. That is all you need to know.'

Yes, Beauty and Truth are here everywhere. Again 'Truth is the consciousness of bliss.°

Another day, another time, maybe someone else will be sitting in this garden, experiencing the wind, the sun, the trees, the beauty of it all. Or maybe, there will be flats here. Whatever. But at this moment, I am here now.

My little cat Sheba, sits curled up sleeping by the sunny wall, unaware of the past or the future, oblivious of the dichotomy of the human being. Erick Fromm said something to the effect of We live knowing that we will die.'

'We can never realise all our potential.° We need other people but we are really always alone.°

I've hardly sat in the garden this summer - so much rain. I've seen less than half a dozen butterflies, and the weeds have taken over this year. But it's still glorious. Oh well, the sun's going in, and so am I.

AUTUMN

The sad raucous cry of crows
Herald Autumn.
A soft, chill mistiness
At early morning.
Dry, brown, wrinkled leaves
Litter the ground.
Geese flying far away
Honking hauntingly.

Clouds skudding, fleetingly.
Sunshine desultory, shadowy.
Evenings closing in,
Flowers fading.
A musty perfume in the air.
A smell of burning wood.
A maturing, a mellowing,
Serenity, surrender, resignation
Autumn

PEACE

I see peace in the tiny baby fast asleep.
Peace in the sheep grazing quietly on the hill.
Peace in the silvery moonlight softly shining down,
As by the weeping willow I stand still.
Peace in the murmuring stream flowing thru' the fields.
Peace in the sweet, fresh, fragrant early morn.
Peace in the diamond dew that sparkles on the grass.
Peace in each pure creature newly born.
Peace in the soft, gentle doves cooing overhead.
Peace in the bright eyed blackbird singing in the tree.
The peace we experience in this world
Reflects the true peace within you, within me.

ELEPHANT 2

The elephant
Is a wonderous sight
Such majesty, such strength,
Such power and such might.

See how he walks his path
With delicate, gentle tread
And see how with infinite grace,
He moves his massive head.

AUTUMN WONDER

Leaves
Falling
  Falling
    Falling
Silently, gently
  Slowly, delicately
    To the earth. Falling
      Floating
      Fluttering

To a thick, crisp carpet
Of gold and orange and brown and red

Each leaf falls
  At its due time.
    Falls
      Falls
        Falls

And returns to the earth
    From whence it came.

SKYSCAPE

At sunrise and sunset every day
A landscape is painted before our eyes.
The artist is sublime, the canvas is vast,
The infinite canopy of the skies.

His colours are drawn from the rainbow,
Mixed freely with clouds and light,
An ever changing tapestry
Put there for our delight.

Translucent blues, green, pale and deep,
Soft rose shot through with gold,
Colours no man on earth could mix.
See the heavenly art unfold.

His medium is the wind and rain,
His brushes, clouds and air.
With that brilliance, beauty and technique,
No Turner can compare.

Sometimes the sky is gently clad,
Sweet hues that softly flow,
Or the effect is dark and dramatic,
Vivid daubs of indigo.

In our galleries, lie paintings that we store,
But soon each celestial landscape will be no more.
Enjoy the beauty *now* while it is here
In seconds darkness falls, and it will disappear.

How many skies have we seen on this earth?
Countless masterpieces in the years from our birth,
Not one the same, gloriously different each day,
How fortunate we are to have passed this way.

COLD WINTER

Cold winter has come,
The days are dark,
The earth is bare,
The trees stand stark.

Swallows have flown,
To a sunnier clime,
Wild, furry animals
Sleep all the time.

The sky is grey,
No flowers appear,
Cold ice and frost,
And snow are near.

All nature's still,
And slow and quiet,
The days are short,
And long each night.

But in my heart,
Still shines the sun,
It's there each hour,
For everyone.

We may not see it
In the sky,
But it's always there
For you and I.

The joy we feel,
The love we know,
Is not dependent
On sun or snow.

TWILIGHT

The hot sultry sun
Has set, has gone
The yellow moon has risen
Silently into the sky.
All is peaceful, cool and gentle,
A bird twitters before sleep,
Childrens' voices at bedtime
Through wide open windows.
A plane hums in the sky.
Then everything is still -
Even the trees.
We sit here in the garden,
Chico and I,
Looking, contemplating.
Enjoying cool air
After the heat of the day
It's getting darker
And trees are silhouetted against the deep sky.

MIAOW

I had a little cat
Her name was Miaow
As I write these words
She's not with me now.

She used to sit on my pillow
As I lay in bed
And purr very softly
As I stroked her head

Her sweet green eyes
Gazed into mine
As a cat
She really was divine

Into my life
She slipped one day
As if from nowhere
A little stray

Her coat was tabby
And grey and white
She would turn little somersaults
For my delight.

OCTOBER

Golden days, golden days, golden days of October,
Gentle and mellow and sweet and slow,
Perfumes of roses, soft breezes blowing,
Trees swaying gracefully to and fro.

Leaves yellow, and orange, and red, and brown,
Dropping so softly to the grass below,
Creating a golden patterned glow,
Blood red sun slowly sinking low.

OUR CAT CHICO

Our cat Chico,
Has a very high IQ.
I see you don't believe me,
Well let me enlighten you.

When the weather's very hot,
In our bath he will sleep,
And while we toss and turn,
From him, there's not a peep.

When the weather's very cold,
He likes the softest, warmest chair,
And when it's temperate,
He will settle anywhere.

Nowhere is sacrosanct,
To our clever cat.
Everywhere is his domain,
And that my friends is that.

WHAT IS IT ALL ABOUT?

Can someone please tell me,
What it is all about,
When a cat wants to come in,
When you've just put him out.

And when he is out,
He wants to come in.
We don't have a cat flap
So it's wearing me thin.

He's in, then he's out.
A plaintive miaow.
°Can you please let me in
And make it right now?'

I'm not a cat therapist.
Of that there's no doubt,
But there must be a reason
Why once in, he wants out!

CATS

Cats can ignore you,
Or may choose to adore you
Cats can irritate,
Or your worries eliminate.

Cats are never fidgety
And keep their dignity.
They have a certain charm
And never cause alarm.

SNOW MAGIC

While I slept, the world was transformed
From colour to black and white.
Whiteness, dazzling, glistening
Immobilising the living trees.

Not a leaf moved, not a branch swayed.
The oak tree, like Lot's wife
Stood petrified
With icicles and icy tears.

The weeping willow, like a radiant bride,
Spread wide her skirts
Of delicate filigree.
And - all was muffled.

It was a magical land
Strange, dreamlike and mystical,
Quiet, and slow, and still,
As if waiting - Waiting.. .

And then - a blackbird sang!
A robin flew on to a twig
With breast of blood, red brightness
Chirping his sweet, sharp song.

The sun beamed out,
And all glimmered in his light.
The fir tree slipped her lacy cover.
And showed her dark green cloak.

In the sky, a little blue corner showed.
And fluffy clouds, pink and grey and white.
The muffled sound of shovels, brooms and spades,
Clear childrens° voices on their way to school.

The milkman jangled his bottles
The sound shattering the still air.
It was clear and bright and gay
A feeling of excitement and expectancy.

LITTLE BIRD

Spread your wings little bird,
And fly off to the sun,
To the sky, to the stars,
'Til the day is done.

Soar higher and higher
In joy and with grace,
Have trust, do not fear,
The pure air is your place.

This is your time now,
To enjoy and to live,
As you sing your sweet song,
What pleasure you give.

Our hearts are uplifted,
By your beautiful flight,
Reach for the stars, joyous bird,
Until it is night.

WALTZING, WALTZING

When I hear the music of Johann Strauss,
I turn up the volume to fill the house.
My toes start to tingle, my head starts to sway;
It banishes all my cares away.

I imagine I'm swirling in dress of lace,
And a handsome stranger looks into my face.
We waltz and we polka, we pirouette,
To the fragrant perfume of mignonette.

With the strains of Blue Danube, I become ecstatic,
And the effect on me is automatic.
Whatever I'm doing, come time or tide,
I pick up the cat, and away we glide.

Across the kitchen and into the hall
We waltz, me and pussy cat, having a ball,
I sing and she purrs, and twirling we flow
Till the music stops and we curtsey low.

THE SEA

O sea serene,
O sparkling sea, supremely silver,
Your monotonous murmur sends
My senses to sleep
Like an angelic choir,
Or a mother's sweet lullaby,
The myriad of soft voices
Of the turquoise deep.

O turbulent sea!
Tossing and turning,
Whipped by the winds,
So strong, so wild!
In total blackness your waves are thrashing,
Unmercifully whipped by gale and storm,
Your unfathomable depths
Are a dim, dark mystery.

SHEBA - 2

Around 6 o'clock, on the stairs, there's a tread,
And a soft furry creature springs on to my bed.
On to my pillow she nestles so neatly,
Always immaculate, smelling so sweetly.
Brown ears and face and thick, creamy fur
Clear blue eyes, brown paws and tail, and a loud purr.
Then, into the kitchen she waits by her dish:
A plaintive: 'Meow! Can I please have my fish?'
O my little cat you are such a treasure,
Of happy moments, you've given full measure.

CONTRASTS

THE LAKE

The fish glide silently, soothingly, gracefully along in their dim, dark peaceful environment.

Swallows, thrushes, blackbirds and myriads of different birds fly constantly high and low, back and forth over the lake, looking for food for their young, materials for their nests, singing and calling to one another.

The waters ripple with bubbles; an occasional insect, frog or beetle disrupts fractionally the deep, dim, dark depths. Above, jewel like dragonflies and brilliant butterflies hover and flutter above the lush, green reeds and stalwart bulrushes. Deep pink water lilies grow here, like lotus flowers, their roots in the muddy, murky water, but their beautiful flowers always rising above to the clear pure air, no matter how high the dirty water rises.

Here come the Canada geese with their three downy babies, hungry always, and the mallards and the mother coot, putting food into the mouths of her little ones.

But with nonchalance and serenity and grace, surrendering in complete confidence, the fish glide on.

THE SWIMMING POOL

Here in a ceaseless cacophony of squeals, humanity desports itself -noisily, awkwardly, in constant motion - Jumping and diving -splintering the clear azure surface. Blue shimmer - joyous activity -shouts and squeals - little squirming, cavorting bodies.

A small figure dives, disappearing into the blue water. It splinters and sprays. It cascades into white foam, and then settles into flowing, glowing, blue active smoothness, like a turquoise jelly with highlights of sunshine.

Screams of joy - wet clad figures dripping. Many voices. Squeals and cries and shouts and yells merge into one seemingly no ending headache - provoking shriek - until suddenly, a piercing whistle yells cuts through the chaos. Then a gradual, gradual dispersal, voices muffled softly and then at last silence.

The water is still, so still.

COLOURS

Rose pink is the colour of my chiffon gown
The colour of love, a baby's soft cheek of down,
The shy blush on the face of a young girl,
And a pink rosebud ready to unfurl.

White is the colour of the sweet bride's dress,
The colour of purity and tenderness.
Fluffy high clouds, gleaming ice and soft snow showers,
A graceful swan's feathers and orange blossom flowers.

Green is the colour to wear in the Spring
The colour of nature that makes the heart sing,
Of leaves, trees and grass and all things that grow
A colour that soothes and calms us so.

Deep blue is the colour called ultramarine,
The colour of healing, so peaceful, serene.
The midnight sky, the Aegean sea.
Paintings by Titian and Botticelli.

Yellow (gold) is the colour of ripening corn,
The colour of daffodils, a chick new born,
Sunflowers, mimosa, buttercups bright
And shimmering sunshine spreading light.

THE RAIN IN SPRING

The rain came pattering down
So gentle and sweet,
Like a heavenly massage
Invigorating and yet so soft.

A little thrush on the fence
Held his speckled breast to the rain,
His feathers fluttered in enjoyment
For the cleansing, gentle rain.

The crocuses and daffodils, half open,
The trees not yet ready to bloom,
But waiting, yes, patiently, for the time
To burst forth, welcomed the rain.

Cars glided by, their noise muffled
By the rain, then - an increase of
momentum,
And I held my face upwards,
Grateful for the healing, heavenly rain.

AUTUMN LEAVES

Dancing leaves
Chasing each other
Down the street.
Playful leaves
Floating and frolicking,
Scurrying and crunching,
Alone and bunching,
Blown by the wind,
And kicked by children,
With squeals of delight.

1ST AUGUST

Early Sunday morning on 1st August.
The air is cool and fresh and fragrant,
It refreshes me.
A new day, a new beginning,
So quiet, so peaceful
The day seems to hold its breath
In quiet expectancy.
Birds singing sweetly,
Soft breezes gently touch my face.
Church bells call in the far distance.

A smell of jasmine, cut grass, honeysuckle,
Dew on the roses,
Cobwebs glow like jewelled diadems.
A magpie chatters,
Wild ducks fly by, necks outstretched,
A joyful sound, so free.
A little Autumnal chill is in the air,
Cherry tree leaves turning red,
I feel blessed by a loving presence
Tender, kindly, divine.

Under the willow tree, the early sun warms me,
I feel enfolded in love and joy
Chico my cat, leaps with life and happiness,
°Chase me, chase me, catch me if you can!'
Everything is growing, flourishing, unfolding
Sunflowers smile at me
And turn their golden faces towards the sun
Thank you, thank you, thank you!

FAREWELL LITTLE ONE

Goodbye my little cat,
I loved you so.
It broke my heart, my little one,
To let you go.
The love you gave so joyously
From your fragile frame,
Has now returned to that Great Love
From which you came.
You taught me so much, little friend,
My stray called Miaow.
You enjoyed each moment of your life,
Lived in the now.
You made me laugh, feel love and joy,
Made my heart lift
The happy years we had with you
Were such a gift.
God made you with such care,
Such charm, such tenderness, such grace,
The sweetest little furry, whiskered
Catty face.
And now you sleep for ever
'Neath the willow tree.
Where in the sunshine we would sit
Just you and me.
My heart is heavy, but I'll not forget
What you gave me.

PURRING

There's a gentle purring sound
As my cat sits on my chest,
There's a lovely burbling sound
From the cat that I know best.

It's such a tranquillising throb
When I can't get off to sleep,
For after a short *treatment*
I drift into the deep.

I wish I could capture that soft purr
And put it in a tin,
So I could take a little,
When I feel tense and worn, and thin.

I would give some to other people
To help them to relax,
Send some over through the telephone,
Some by letter or by fax.

Instead of taking valium
To keep themselves quite calm,
They could stroke a cat, and hear him purr,
And enjoy nature's healing balm.

BUTTERFLY

The Butterfly,
Symbol of joy and resurrection,
Is born as a grub,
And just eats and eats and eats and eats.
And as a Caterpillar,
A crawling, earth bound creature,
Munches on cabbages and mulberry leaves,
Getting fatter, and fatter, and fatter, and
fatter
Until his skin splits and bursts, and splits
again.

But, he knows the right time to cease,
And spin his fragile cocoon of silk,
And there he will stay in the stillness,
No eating, no movement -
Waiting, waiting -
And in the darkness,
A transformation is taking place,
A miracle of creation.
For from the Cocoon's womb
A movement, a happening -
And a creatures emerges,
Trembling, delicate,
And lifts his antennae to the sky.
Wings! - Yes wings!
Tremble and flutter,
And open wide and wider.
He rests a while,
And behold!
A creature of great beauty,
Colour translucent, red and blue and gold,
Miraculous rebirth!
And then, like gossamer he flies!
And delicately drinks nectar from a rose.

Grub, Caterpillar, Cocoon, Butterfly -
How did the Grub become the
Butterfly?

28TH FEBRUARY

Nearly spring!
I can see daffodils
About to burst forth with golden
trumpets
Like an orchestra.
Nearly spring!
And forsythia
A mass of bright yellow,
Crocuses, mauve and white,
Bravely thrusting through the earth.
Plum and cherry blossom
Have suddenly appeared,
A miracle of delicate pink and white.
Little green buds on the willow,
The first tree in my garden to leaf.
'Oh how I've missed you
This long, dark, cold winter'
Nearly spring!
Now birds are singing
A wonderful dawn chorus.
There is a rhythm, a dance,
A quickening of life.
A fragrance, a gentle music,
A freshness, an awakening,
That lifts our hearts,
Nearly spring